ESTABLISHED

*Growing In Your Walk With Christ:
Companion Workbook*

JACK E. NEWTON

*Therefore, as you received Christ Jesus the Lord, so walk in him, rooted and built up in him
and established in the faith, just as you were taught, abounding in thanksgiving.*
Colossians 2:6-7

No portion of this material can be reproduced, copied, shared, recorded or otherwise manipulated or distributed without the written consent of the author.
Copyright ã 2019

Scripture quotations are from The ESV® Bible (The Holy Bible, English Standard Version®), copyright © 2001 by Crossway, a publishing ministry of Good News Publishers. Used by permission. All rights reserved.

Dragonfly Press

Dallas, Texas
www.dragonflypress.org

ISBN# 9780998940526

CONTENTS

Acknowledgements vii
Overview: Companion Workbook xi
Introduction: Established and Built Up xv

Chapter 1   Understanding Your Salvation 1

Part I   Nourishment
Chapter 2   Quiet Time 11
Chapter 3   Private Prayer 27
Chapter 4   Hindrances to Private Prayer 38
Chapter 5   Bible Study (Observation) 47
Chapter 6   Bible Study (Interpretation) 54
Chapter 7   Bible Study (Application) 63

Part II   Community
Chapter 8   Church Membership 74
Chapter 9   Purpose of the Church 78
Chapter 10   Church Discipline 86
Chapter 11   Corporate Prayer 89
Chapter 12   Worship 99

Part II   Community

Chapter 13 Evangelism 106

Chapter 14 Ministry 121

End Notes 127

About the Author 133

ACKNOWLEDGEMENTS

I am eternally grateful for the many people who have poured their lives into me over the years. This is my opportunity to give back. Through the discipleship of others and the lordship of Jesus, I have been able to glean this teaching that has already helped many Christians grow. We all stand on one another's shoulders, but we will only endure if Jesus is our foundation.

I am thankful for those who invested in me. It's up to each of us to find someone into whom we may invest our lives. Spiritual growth isn't for the sake of growth alone. It's for the advancement of the Kingdom of God.

There are three groups of people I would like to thank for influencing me, and this book. The first is for my siblings and their spouses. You knew me before I came to know the Lord and even though it wasn't easy you didn't give up on me. The Lord knows I gave you ample reason to write me off and yet you helped me, prayed for me, encouraged me, and told me the right things, which aren't always the easy things. I wouldn't be where I am today without your help and love.

The second group, are those Pastors, teachers, professors, and encouragers who God placed in my life since I came to know Him. God's plan is for His people to invest their lives into each other as they grow in Him. To list each one of you would be too long and I'm afraid that I would inadvertently miss some deserving of gratitude. I'm aware that I, like all of us, am standing on the shoulders of others. Those of you who have picked me up and dusted me off in my journey are amazing and loving Christians who challenge me every day to be the man God created me to be.

JACK E. NEWTON

Finally, I want to thank my family. Jon and Amber, you are examples of passionate and humble servants of the Lord. Sam and Lindsey, your wisdom in Christ inspires and challenges me to be better and grow in Him. Leah and Zach, the love you have for the Lord, each other, and your family is an example for me to follow. Dana, I don't have enough words to express what you are to me. You know. Let me call you sweetheart…

For Jackson, Asa, Jude, Selah, Owen…

OVERVIEW

COMPANION WORKBOOK

Everyone then who hears these words of mine and does them will be like a wise man who built his house on the rock. - Matthew 7:24

It isn't enough to know what to do. We must be willing to put those things into practice. When the "rains" and the "winds" of life come, as they inevitably do, will they find us built on the firm foundation of obedience to God and growth in Him? Are we being established in the faith?

The purpose of this workbook is to accompany the volume, *Established: Growing in Your Walk with Christ,* so we may apply the principles and live them out. This workbook is a resource to facilitate growth. Therefore, take time to examine and utilize each aspect included within these pages. You will learn and grow in proportion to the effort you give.

AN EFFECTIVE AND REWARDING PROCESS

There are three things you can do to help make this a more effective and rewarding process.

1. <u>Prayer</u>
   Christian growth isn't merely an act of the will; it's a spiritual process. Therefore, pray for God's help as you work through this study, prayerfully considering each answer and each exercise. Avoid the temptation to fill in the blanks without consulting the Lord. As you consult Him, God may

2. Invite Others

   Invite others to take this journey with you. It's always helpful to have a companion in any endeavor. This is especially true with our Christian walk. Find someone with whom you can be accountable and share your struggles and victories. It's important to understand that we are responsible for each other. This is more than a hobby; it's the very life of our spiritual walk. Share it with others.

3. Spiritual Journal

   A journal will be an invaluable accessory to this study, allowing you to write questions and concerns. It will provide extra space to address issues, help you organize your thoughts, and process difficult principles. Writing often helps with clarifying and illuminating thoughts and ideas. A journal will also document your spiritual journey, which can be an encouragement and resource in the future.

EXERCISES

To reap the benefits of each chapter in the volume, *Established: Growing in Your Walk With Christ*, exercises are given in this companion workbook for reflection, meditation, and action. The exercises aren't an exhaustive list for spiritual growth, and you're encouraged to follow the Lord's leading in response to the lessons. If the exercises are overwhelming, pick one or two, and work through them diligently and completely. These are growth tools and should be used as the Lord leads.

ADDITIONAL RESOURCES

Many chapters have additional resources, which are often examples, guides, or further information for implementing the principles taught. At the end of the workbook you will find a bibliography / suggested reading list. The purpose of this section is twofold. First, to credit those who have influenced this work. Second, to encourage you to develop the habit of reading good books. The books on this list deal with issues addressed in this study. It isn't an exhaustive list, but it's a good place to start.

ENJOY THE JOURNEY

God is faithful and desires to use you in wonderful and powerful ways. There's no more rewarding and fulfilling life than the one lived for Christ. Remember, you are not alone. God will provide others to help you along the way. Most importantly, Jesus told us He will be with us every step of the way (Matthew 28:20b; Hebrews 13:5). Let's grow with Him together as He establishes us in an unshakable faith. Remember, the wise man built his house upon the rock.

There is a joy in the journey, there's a light we can love on the way.
There is wonder and wildness to life, and freedom for those who obey.
<u>Joy in the Journey</u>, Michael Card [1]

INTRODUCTION

ESTABLISHED AND BUILT UP

Therefore, as you received Christ Jesus the Lord, so walk in him rooted and built up in him and established in the faith, just as you were taught, abounding in thanksgiving. Colossians 2:6-7

According to Colossians 2:6-7 (above), what is necessary for a Christian to be "established" in the faith?

What does it mean to be "rooted" in Christ? Why is this important in the life of a believer?

According to the grace of God given to me, like a skilled master builder I laid a foundation, and someone else is building upon it. Let each one take care how he builds upon it. For no one can lay a foundation other than that which is laid, which is Jesus Christ. 1 Corinthians 3:10-11

According to I Corinthians 3:10-11 (above), what does it mean to be "built up" in Christ? Who does the building? Why is this important?

This book and workbook are intended for the following:

- New believers
- Believers who haven't grown
- Believers who have stopped growing
- Believers seeking to help others

Where are you in your walk with Christ? If you're a believer, are you growing? Why or why not? If you are unsure about what it means to be a believer in Christ, refer to the next chapter of this workbook, Understanding Your Salvation, which will explain the plan of salvation and show the next steps in becoming a believer.

It's important to understand the first book along with this workbook will be helpful to those who already have a relationship with the Lord. It's also important to understand that God creates unique relationships according to His Word. Therefore, when we pursue an intimate relationship with Him, our relationship isn't a duplicate of someone else's. For example, my prayer time may be different from yours. Only God can bring this about. We aren't clones, robots or puppets.

How would you describe your relationship with God?

A relationship with God is based in love, not legalism. Therefore, it would be a mistake to think, *'If I do certain things, then God is obligated to bless me.'* The motivation of a growing Christian is one of love for God. This love drives us to develop a more intimate relationship with Him. Legalism depends on the work of people, while grace only comes from God.

Are there areas in your life that fall under legalism rather than love?

EXERCISES

1. Begin a journal to record questions and issues that you want to address in the future.

CHAPTER 1

UNDERSTANDING YOUR SALVATION

*For God so loved the world that He gave His only begotten Son,
that whoever believes in Him should not perish but have everlasting life. John 3:16*

THE PLAN OF SALVATION

If you are uncertain about your relationship with God, please read and consider what He is saying to you in this explanation of salvation.

The Gospel begins with an understanding of sin. Everyone is a sinner, "For all have sinned and fall short of the glory of God" (Romans 3:23). This means everyone has done something wrong and fall below God's standard of perfection. It's easy to compare ourselves to other people. You might look pretty good compared to me, but this isn't the standard. We must compare ourselves to the sinless perfection of God. When we do, it's easy to see we don't measure up.

Next, sin comes with a penalty. Scripture says, "The wages of sin is death" (Romans 6:23). Death in the Bible is separation from God. It includes separation here on earth, where we are unable to find the fulfillment and purpose for which we were created. It also includes separation in eternity. A wage is something we earn. When we allow sin into our lives, we earn death.

Here's the good news! God understands our predicament. We are sinners, and our sin separates us from Him. No matter how many good works we do, we cannot wash away our sin. This is where God stepped in and provided a way. He loves us so much, He came to the earth as a man to take our place (John 3:16). If death comes because of sin, then why did Jesus die? He had no sin. He was perfect and sinless. The answer is, He took our place. He took our punishment.

Well, most people have heard that Jesus died for our sins. What they often don't understand is, just knowing about Jesus isn't enough. The Bible says even the demons believe God exists (James 2:19). Salvation is about more than merely believing God exists. It's about responding in faith to the offer of salvation God has provided through Jesus. God loves you and wants you to find forgiveness and new life in Him.

The Sinner's Prayer

Only a faith response to the Gospel message results in eternal life. Good works (religion, charity, piety…) won't save us. Only faith in Jesus Christ results in a personal relationship with Him. The sinner's prayer is a powerful way you can respond and accept the Gospel message of Jesus. These aren't "magic words," but are words that can be used to respond to the Gospel.

Dear God,

I know I'm a sinner. I have done many wrong things. My sin separates me from you. I also know You love me and You showed Your love when Jesus died on the cross. Today I believe with my heart and confess with my mouth that Jesus is my Savior and Lord. Thank you for loving me and providing this forgiveness and eternal life I couldn't provide for myself. May my life bring glory to You. In Jesus name. Amen.

Celebrate and Share Your Decision

If you prayed the sinner's prayer today and placed your faith in Christ, briefly journal about your decision to follow Christ, include today's date, and celebrate your decision by sharing this good news with someone.

The Transforming Power of Salvation

> *Besides this you know the time, that the hour has come for you to wake from sleep. For salvation is nearer to us now than when we first believed. Romans 13:11*

If salvation is only a prayer we prayed a long time ago, how can the Bible teach that salvation is nearer now than when we first believed?

> *Therefore, my beloved, as you have always obeyed, so now, not only as in my presence but much more in my absence, <u>work out your own salvation</u> with fear and trembling. Philippians 2:12*

In Philippians 2:12, what does scripture mean to "work out our salvation?" Are we responsible for earning our salvation?

Like newborn infants, long for the pure spiritual milk, that by it you may <u>grow up into salvation.</u>
1 Peter 2:2

In 1 Peter 2:2, what does the Scripture mean that we are to grow up into salvation? Do we have to somehow make ourselves acceptable to God before He will save us?

Past: We Were Saved

Sin includes anything we do contrary to God's will. Sin is something each of us commits, and sin has dire consequences.

According to Romans 6:23, what is the consequence of sin? What does it mean to be born again?

Over the years the term "born again Christian" has become a negative title. This is partly due to the unchristian way many Christians have acted, and partly due to the negative way the world views Christianity. Many Christians have shied away from this term and the doctrine behind it. This is a mistake. A proper understanding of our salvation begins with the understanding, as believers, we are born again. Without regeneration, there is no life or growth in Christ.

Regeneration

When God gives His new life to us, He desires to use us to bring others to Himself. This can only happen when others see the difference He makes in our life. It's the work of God in us that transforms us into the person He created us to be. He's the one who saves. He is the one who transforms. He's the one who gets the glory for it all.

> *And you were dead in the trespasses and sins in which you once walked, following the course of this world, following the prince of the power of the air, the spirit that is now at work in the sons of disobedience — among whom we all once lived in the passions of our flesh, carrying out the desires of the body and the mind, and were by nature children of wrath, like the rest of mankind. But God, being rich in mercy, because of the great love with which he loved us, even when we were dead in our trespasses, made us alive together with Christ — by grace you have been saved. Ephesians 2:1-5*

> *Therefore, if anyone is in Christ, he is a new creation The old has passed away; behold, the new has come. 2 Corinthians 5:17*

According to the scriptures above, what is regeneration?

Why is regeneration an important part of understanding our salvation?

What makes regeneration necessary?

What are some principles that help us understand the need for regeneration?

What are some scriptures addressing the topic of regeneration?

Present: We Are Being Saved

Often, as Christians, we look at our spiritual growth and become satisfied and complacent. We justify such times of self-satisfaction as an earned respite from the rigors of the sanctification process. There's no such thing as a spiritual plateau. The Christian life is like swimming upstream. We convince ourselves we have made great progress and deserve to tread water for a while. What we don't realize is, while we are treading water, we are being swept downstream. If we aren't growing in our faith, we are declining. This continued growth is essential in our understanding of the process of sanctification, which changes Christians for a lifetime.

For we are his workmanship, created in Christ Jesus for good works, which God prepared beforehand, that we should walk in them. Ephesians 2:10

Briefly describe the process of sanctification?

For this is the will of God, your sanctification: that you abstain from sexual immorality; that each one of you know how to control his own body in holiness and honor, not in the passion of lust like the Gentiles who do not know God. 1 Thessalonians 4:3-5

What does it mean that we are being changed over our lifetime?

What is the difference between regeneration and sanctification?

And we all, with unveiled face, beholding the glory of the Lord, are being transformed into the same image from one degree of glory to another. For this comes from the Lord who is the Spirit. 2 Corinthians 3:18

What is the danger of the idea of "treading water" in our walk with Christ?

Future: We will be Saved

> *Now it was so, when Moses came down from Mount Sinai (and the two tablets of the Testimony were in Moses' hand when he came down from the mountain), that Moses did not know that the skin of his face shone while he talked with Him. Exodus 34:29*

When Moses came down from the mountain, his face shone with the reflected glory of God. When the people saw it, they hid in fear. This is the best example of a human showing God's glory. According to Romans 3:23, our sins keep us from His glory. Even regenerate people struggle with the presence of sin, and if we claim to be without sin, we are liars (1 John 1:8-10).

> *Now after six days Jesus took Peter, James, and John his brother, led them up on a high mountain by themselves; and He was transfigured before them. His face shone like the sun, and His clothes became as white as the light. Matthew 17:1-2*

God has all of the glory and it belongs to Him because He is sinless, pure, righteous and holy. In short, because He is God. At His transfiguration Jesus gave His disciples a glimpse of His glory (Matthew 17:1-2). They were so impacted, all they could do was fall on the ground and hide their faces.

What is glorification and when will it happen?

What is encouraging about the instant glorification of believers?

What will be the ultimate end of believers?

How does a complete understanding of salvation change your view of life and the role of the believer in the world?

JACK E. NEWTON

Explain Romans 13:11, Philippians 2:12-13, and 1 Peter 2:2 in your own words.

> *Besides this you know the time, that the hour has come for you to wake from sleep. For salvation is nearer to us now than when we first believed.*
> *Romans 13:11*

> *Therefore, my beloved, as you have always obeyed, so now, not only as in my presence but much more in my absence, work out your own salvation with fear and trembling.*
> *Philippians 2:12-13*

> *Like newborn infants, long for the pure spiritual milk, that by it you may grow up into salvation.*
> *1 Peter 2:2*

For Christians, salvation is more than our ticket to heaven. When we understand that our salvation consists of an instantaneous regeneration (past), a lifetime process of sanctification (present), and the culmination in instant glorification (future) of believers, we begin to experience the abundant life Christ died to give.

CHAPTER 2

Quiet Time

And this is eternal life, that they may know You, the only true God,
and Jesus Christ, whom You have sent. John 17:3

Whether we call it a personal devotion time, morning watch, Quiet Time, or some other title is irrelevant. What matters most is making this time an important part of our daily life. Our salvation is centered in an ongoing, intimate relationship with God. In order for our relationship to flourish, we need to spend time with Him, making this an important part of our daily life. The more we know Him, the more we open ourselves to His leadership, and the more we see our lives transformed by Him.

Our Quiet Time consists of two primary elements: prayer and Bible study. We will look closely at these two elements in subsequent chapters. So for now, we will examine other elements helpful to our daily Quiet Time.

OTHER QUIET TIME ELEMENTS

WORSHIP

Worship is an outpouring of our lives to God as we see Him working in us. It means to recognize the worth of God as we come before Him in adoration and praise.

JACK E. NEWTON

Find the following scriptures and write them in the space provided:

Genesis 24:26

Exodus 4:31

John 4:24

What are the similarities of these verses?

Are there elements from these examples of worship that you can incorporate into your daily Quiet Time?

Praise

Praise is recognizing the attributes of God. It's acknowledging God for who He is. Praise issues from our heart as we come to know the One who loves and died for us. Praise helps us keep things in perspective and helps us continue to pursue the knowledge of the One who is too great to completely comprehend.

Read Psalm 150, which is a hymn of praise. What are ways and reasons this Psalm says we can praise God? Who is to praise the Lord? For additional study, review Psalm 148 and Psalm 149.

Are there elements from these examples of praise that you can incorporate into your daily Quiet Time?

Fasting

Fasting is an element often overlooked and forgotten by Christians and is a powerful way to come before God in our weakness and find His strength. Fasting is a spiritual process of surrender to God. In Scripture, many of the people God used in special ways, fasted.

JACK E. NEWTON

Look up the following verses and describe the circumstances around each fast. Try to answer some of these questions for each: Who fasted? Why did they fast? How long did they fast? For additional study, you can read further to determine the outcome/result of their fast.

2 Samuel 12:1-23

1 Kings 19:4-8

Acts 9:1-9

Did the above exercise show you anything new about fasting?

Before deciding to fast, please read **The Basics of Fasting** below, and make sure to consult a physician before starting a fast.

The Basics of Fasting

Why do we fast? When we fast, we realize He is the powerful God and we are weak human beings.

How do we fast? An easy way to start is to do a one day (24-hour) fast. For example, start on a given day after the evening meal (6:30 p.m.), then go without food through the night and the next day until breaking the fast by eating the evening meal (6:30 p.m.).

What does fasting accomplish? Going without food isn't as important as how the time during the fast is used. When you feel hunger, take the opportunity to meditate on God. Communicate with Him about why He is more important than physical nourishment.

What if you are unable to fast? Because of medical conditions (or other reasons), many people aren't able to go 24 hours without food. It may be helpful to sacrifice something else (sugar, TV, internet, etc.) to be reminded of God's importance in your life. (Note: Please don't start a fast without consulting a physician.)

Solitude and Silence

We are conditioned to constant background noise, whether in the car, at work, or sleeping. Yet, there is value in occasionally separating from the hustle, bustle, and din of this modern world.

Jesus separated Himself for times of intimacy with His Father. Read the following verses and journal your thoughts on why Jesus withdrew and went to a solitary place.

JACK E. NEWTON

Matthew 14:1-13

Luke 5:12-16

John 6:10-15

How do these examples influence your understanding of the need and conditions for Solitude and Silence?

Read Psalm 46:10. Why should a Christian learn to be still?

Sacrifice

Read Luke 9:23-25. Jesus said if we are to follow Him, we must take up our cross daily. What does this statement mean in your faith journey?

Read Matthew 5:16. What happens when we live for Christ rather than self?

How do these examples influence your understanding of the need and conditions for Sacrifice?

Journaling

Journaling can be done anytime, anywhere, and can be done on computers, tablets, legal pads, notebooks, composition books, or leather-bound journals.

In journaling, there are a few things to keep in mind.

1. This is a record of communication between you and God. Make certain you feel secure enough to write the innermost thoughts and feelings of your life. (Note: Personally, I make it clear that others aren't invited to read my journal. While I don't keep secrets from my wife, the rest of the world is prohibited.)

2. Your journal is your tool for spiritual growth. It shouldn't be a burden. Don't feel you must write ten pages every day. Just use it as it seems good and helpful.

3. Writing can be a healthy and safe outlet for frustrations and anger, allowing you to vent your frustrations to God without any negative consequences. (Note: In the past, I have written angry letters in my journal. I never intended to send them to the addressee. It was just an effective way to deal with my frustrations. After the frustration left, I often destroyed those journal pages.)

4. Journaling is a wonderful way to look back and see the prayers God has answered. It's also a great way to see our progress in spiritual growth. This testimony would be unavailable if we didn't journal.

Some people find a journaling format helpful. Below is a format others have used. Simply fill in the blanks as you go through your Quiet Time.

BIBLE STUDY

Passage:

Passage theme:

Observations:

Interpretation:

Applications:

Prayer Time

Things worthy of praising God:

Things worthy of thanking God:

Things to confess:

Those in need of salvation:

Those who are sick:

Personal needs:

OVERCOMING HINDRANCES

We live in a world of activity and distractions. We have demands from work and family. Responsibilities and obligations constantly tug at us. We have cell phones, texts, and emails to answer. We "must" check our Facebook page or Twitter feed and make sure we are up to date with our favorite TV shows. These distractions hinder our ability to focus on God. How often does our phone buzz just as we open the Bible to read? How often do we think about the email we forgot to answer, or someone knocks on our door, just as we kneel to pray? Sometimes we must battle to make time to concentrate on God. Here are some ways we can win this battle.

Quiet Time Closet

When we want to develop a more intimate marriage, we go away with our spouse. To have a closer relationship with our children, we spend time with them. The same is true in our relationship with God. To love Him is to spend time with Him. Scripture helps us understand how to avoid the noise and distractions that often hinder our time alone with God.

Read the following verses. What do they teach in regards to avoiding distractions in your quiet time?

Psalm 46:10

Matthew 6:5-6

A friend recently showed me her Quiet Time closet. It was her easy chair in the living room of her house. She had all of the necessary tools easily accessible (Bible, journal, hymnal, prayer list, devotional books, pens, reading glasses, journal…). This way she was able to use her time wisely to concentrate solely on God. Wherever we choose to spend our time with God, we can follow her example.

Where do you spend your time with God each day?

Is the place a help or distraction to your Quiet Time? How? If it's a distraction, where could you move?

Baby Steps

One of the funniest movies of all time (in my opinion) is titled, "What About Bob?" In this movie, Bob drives his psychiatrist to a straight jacket by following the doctor's advice. In trying to rid himself of Bob, his psychiatrist tells him to take "baby steps." As Bob takes these baby steps, things begin to work out for him. It's just a movie, but the principle is sound. Especially when it comes to our Quiet Time. Start small.

Why are we reluctant to start small?

Cumulative Effect

A few years ago, I looked in the mirror and didn't like what was looking back at me. I was 55 years old and 80 pounds overweight. I was on all sorts of medications and as weak as a kitten. It was breathtaking just to get on the floor to play with my grandsons. Golf, my lifelong avocation, was almost more than I could accomplish. I set a goal to lose 40 pounds in one year.

I joined a gym, took healthy dietary supplements, changed my diet to healthy foods, and believed I could change. It was difficult and it didn't happen overnight. Two years later and 75 pounds lighter, I was stronger (I even won a few medals in powerlifting), and healthier due to the changes made to my daily schedule. How did I lose 75 pounds? One pound at a time. One decision at a time. One sacrifice at a time. Many days I wanted a piece of cake rather than a salad or fruit. True, one piece of cake would not kill me, but over time, the choices and decisions add up. There is no quick fix to weight loss and gaining strength. There is no magic pill for spiritual growth. Both take time and commitment.

It is rewarding to hear someone say, "Man! You have lost a ton of weight. You look great!" How much more rewarding to hear someone say, "I have been watching you and I see you are really growing in the Lord. How can I have what you have?" These changes only happen when we put in the time, over time. A house is built one brick at a time and a tree adds one ring each year. Christians grow over time as we commit ourselves to the Lord.

What's one thing you can do to build your relationship with Christ? What's stopping you?

Temptations to Give Up

Never give up. Wherever we are, we pick ourselves up, dust ourselves off, and get back to doing what we know is right. There will always be a little voice saying, "This may be for others but it isn't for you." It will tell us, "You're too weak." It will chide, "You're unworthy of an intimate relationship with God." Don't listen to that voice; it's a liar. This is a spiritual battle, so we rely on God to give us strength and trust Him to deliver us from our adversary. God desires to know us and interact with us intimately. We can only fail if we fail to continue.

Why are we often tempted to give up?

What are some of the things that distract you?

What are some of the internal lies you hear telling you to give up?

EXERCISES

1. Schedule your Quiet Time for each day and spend time with the Lord.

2. Read the Bible each day and journal questions or insights you have about your reading.

3. Make a list of people to pray for each day. Add to your list as God brings people to mind.

4. Journal any Quiet Time distractions and hindrances and ask God to help you overcome them. (Be sure to silence electronics.)

5. Journal any struggles you have in maintaining a consistent Quiet Time each day. Pray for God's help to continue.

6. If you are deemed physically capable of fasting, consider periodically incorporating this into your life as part of your fellowship with God. (Consult a physician before fasting.)

CHAPTER 3

PRIVATE PRAYER

Private prayer, at its core, is concerned with an intimate relationship between God and us. Prayer is talking to, communing with, worshiping, having intimacy with, relating to, and loving God. Prayer is also God talking to, communing with, accepting worship from, being intimate with, relating to, and loving us. It's a two-way communication between God and people, which builds the trust and relationship between them. God desires to communicate with us, and prayer is the vehicle that takes us into His presence.

Often our time with God is spent learning about Him without getting to know Him. Years ago, I knew a woman who boasted about how long she spent in prayer. She sought approval and wanted to be known as a "prayer warrior." What she didn't understand was, her time in prayer was supposed to be about growing closer to God, seeking His approval and needing His presence in her life. In bringing this to the attention of others, she was trying to attain from others what could only come from God. We deprive ourselves of the reward of knowing God when we are more concerned with what others think (Matthew 6:5-6).

Why are we often concerned about obtaining the approval of people?

Prayer in the Old Testament: Daniel

In Daniel 6:10-11, a young Jewish man named Daniel was an outsider, elevated to power in the Persian Empire. The Persian leaders were jealous of the way God blessed Daniel by giving him favor with the king. They knew of Daniel's commitment to prayer, so they set a trap. They played to the vanity of the King and had him sign a decree, stating anyone praying to anyone or anything other than the King would be throw into the lions' den. This limitation on prayer lasted thirty days.

Daniel knew the risk of continuing to kneel before God three times a day, but his time with God was more important than his own life.

Because of his disregard of the decree and his regard for God, Daniel was thrown in the lions' den.

How important is prayer to you? Are you willing to risk going to jail if a similar law was passed in our land? Explain.

Prayer in the Old Testament: David

In Psalm 55:17, David writes, "Evening and morning and at noon, I utter my complaint and moan, and he hears my voice." David prayed all during the day because he desired an intimate relationship with God. He asked for God's advice and direction in the decisions he made as king.

Are you comfortable praying? Are you satisfied with your prayer life? How often during the day do you pray?

For further study and a rich record of private personal prayers in the Old Testament, read the following:

Abram's interaction with God before the destruction of Sodom and Gomorrah
Genesis 18:22-33

The prayer of Abraham's servant as he went to find a wife for Isaac
Genesis 24

The prayers of Elijah
1 Kings 18

In each of the examples above, what was the main purpose for prayer? How did God answer? How was the relationship with God shown through the prayer and God's answer?

Prayer in the New Testament

In Matthew 6:7, Jesus said, "When you pray," not "If you pray." He assumed prayer would be part of the Christian's life, and He made prayer a priority.

John 17 is known as Jesus' high priestly prayer. In this prayer, we get a glimpse into the relationship and communication Jesus has with the Father. His concern for the glory of the Father and His compassion for those around Him are touching and convicting, as well as His prayer for those who would subsequently become believers due to the witness of His disciples.

We have the wonderful privilege of listening in on the prayer of Jesus as He prepares for the cross. That same evening in the Garden of Gethsemane, He prayed for God's will to be done in His life as He obediently went to the cross.

Prayer cannot be ignored if we are to grow in our walk with Christ the way He wants us to. The Bible contains many examples and teachings on prayer. Suffice it to say, prayer is essential to all we do. Without it, we are groping in the dark, hoping to find something that is impossible to grasp.

Read the three prayers of Jesus found in John 17:1-26.
John 17:1-5. Jesus prays for Himself.

John 17:6-19. Jesus prays for His disciples.

John 17:20-26. Jesus prays for future believers.

What do you think was the main purpose of each prayer?

Are there elements from these examples of prayer you can incorporate into your daily quiet time?

Patterns for Private Prayer

It's easy to stray from our original intention when we bow to pray. We often find ourselves after an hour, no closer to God than when we began, and our prayers sound something like this: "Dear God. I … I … I … Me … Me … Me … Now … Now … Now … Amen." We fall into the trap of making our prayer life about us and not about God or others. In such prayers, we aren't seeking Him. We are using our prayer time to dictate our demands to God. In this case, we fall into idolatry of self. We are in charge; we're the authority; we know best. God isn't going to share His throne or glory with anyone (Isaiah 42:8). He loves us and desires to commune with us. But we must understand He is God and we aren't.

How does the pattern of prayer: Praise, Thanksgiving, Confession, Intercession and Supplication keep our priorities in order and focus on what is important?

Praise

When we praise God, we recognize the greatness of God. Such praise fulfills us in a way nothing else can. Starting our prayers with praise helps us make sure we are concentrating on God and the things of God. This is what Jesus taught in the beginning of the Lord's Prayer.

> *Our Father in heaven, hallowed be your name. Matthew 6:9*

God knows He is in heaven and He knows His name is holy. When we praise Him, we aren't informing Him of something He doesn't already know. We are agreeing with Him that He is who He says He is. Praise begins our prayer time in a different way than with our self-centered prayers.

How does praise shift the focus from self to God?

Thanksgiving

Give thanks in all circumstances; for this is the will of God in Christ Jesus for you.
1 Thessalonians 5:18

Thanksgiving is an important element in our prayers because it causes us to realize how much God has done.

How does thanksgiving shift the focus from our needs to God?

Confession

Often, we get so busy doing good works, we forget the Christian walk is about who we are, and not just the things we do. Confession helps us be honest with God and ourselves. When we practice confession, we see how our sin is grievous in the sight of God.

JACK E. NEWTON

If we say we have no sin, we deceive ourselves, and the truth is not in us. If we confess our sins, he is faithful and just to forgive us our sins and to cleanse us from all unrighteousness. If we say we have not sinned, we make him a liar, and his word is not in us. 1 John 1:8-10

What is the role of confession in our daily life?

How does confession keep our tendency toward prideful living in check?

What are the dangers in ignoring confession?

Repentance is necessary for God to continue the process of sanctification in us. Therefore, it's important that we don't neglect confession in prayer. When we practice confession, we see how our sin is grievous in the sight of God.

Intercession

Intercession is a part of our prayers where we stand in the gap for others who are lost or hurting. It's focused on the needs of others. True prayers for others flow from a genuine heart of desire for their wellbeing. We must be careful not to use the time of building our prayer list as a time of gossip with others and with God.

> *Is anyone among you suffering? Let him pray. Is anyone cheerful? Let him sing praise. Is anyone among you sick? Let him call for the elders of the church, and let them pray over him, anointing him with oil in the name of the Lord. And the prayer of faith will save the one who is sick, and the Lord will raise him up. And if he has committed sins, he will be forgiven. James 5:13-15*

What is the role of intercession in our prayer life?

How does intercession keep our focus in prayer toward God rather than self?

Supplication

> *Give us this day our daily bread. And lead us not into temptation, but deliver us from evil. Matthew 6:11, 13*

Supplication occurs when we cry out for God to intervene and provide in our own lives or our church. There's nothing wrong with praying for our personal needs. The problem comes when we treat God like a bubblegum machine. This is poor theology and shortchanges us from experiencing the blessings resulting from an intimate relationship with God.

> *You ask and do not receive, because you ask wrongly, to spend it on your passions. James 4:3*

Have you, now or in the past, treated God like a bubblegum machine, putting in your request and expecting Him to pop out the right answer?

Do you recognize other areas of "poor theology" that govern your life or the lives of others? Explain.

Our heavenly Father knows our needs, He knows what we have done, and He knows what needs to happen in our lives.

When I was a child, I lied to my mom. The fact that I lied bothered me. Finally, one night I confessed to her I had lied.

She said, "I know."

"If you already knew, then why didn't you say something? I haven't been able to eat or sleep and my life has been miserable!"

She responded "Because you needed to come to me and make it right."

We need to come to Him. We need to cry out to our Abba, which is an intimate term a child uses for their father, and ask Him to take care of us. When we cry out to Him, He hears us and, as a loving Father, He takes care of us.

Many years ago, a popular bumper sticker stated, "God is my copilot." When we truly understand prayer and interact with Him in an intimate way, we begin to realize God is our PILOT. We are His sheep and He is our shepherd.

Why are we so reluctant to rely upon God?

EXERCISES

1. During your Quiet Time, pray through the prayer pattern of Praise, Thanksgiving, Confession, Intercession and Supplication.

2. Are there other patterns of prayer you find useful in your private prayer time? Are there elements mentioned in this study you can incorporate into your prayer time with God?

3. As you talk to God, listen for Him to speak and lead. Enjoy the fellowship with Him.

4. Continue your conversation with God all day. Was this difficult for you? Why?

5. Continue to pray for the people on your prayer list.

CHAPTER 4

HINDRANCES TO PRIVATE PRAYER

Our relationship with God is built over time. As with any spiritual exercise, there are obstacles to accomplishing the will of God. We have an adversary who is constantly fighting against our growth in God. Satan is actively working to make sure we remain prayerless. We cannot blame him for our lack of power, however. We are each responsible for our own actions and inactions. Though none of us will do this perfectly, we must be prepared to fight the battle of distraction. This is a fight God can win through us.

Some things occur in our lives that hinder our prayer relationship with God. These include distraction, sleep, pride, repetition and sin.

DISTRACTION

Have you attempted to talk on the telephone while someone in the same room is asking you a question? You try to hear both conversations at once but end up hearing neither. To make sense of the situation, you must ask one of the people to hold while you talk to the other. As you listen to each in turn, you can handle each situation.

The idea we are at our best when multi-tasking is false. We are much better when we can concentrate on one thing at a time. While it's not always an option at work or home, we can make it happen in our personal prayer time.

Have you tried to pray and found your mind wandering to other things?

How can you harness these wandering thoughts so your focus stays on God?

SLEEP

Sleep is perpetually a hindrance to prayer. It's common as we settle into a Quiet Time so we can concentrate on God and pray, to find we have fallen asleep.

Take a look at the battle between sleep and prayer (Matthew 26:40,43). If you find yourself losing the battle to sleep, how can you reschedule your prayer time so you become the victor?

Pride

We don't like to ask for help because we feel it's admitting we can't handle the situation. We don't like to confess sin because it shows we are flawed.

In Isaiah 42:8, we read that God is not going to share His glory with anyone or anything. Read James 4:10. How can you battle against pride becoming an idol in your life?

Repetition

When I was a child, I learned little poem prayers. "God is great. God is good. Let us thank Him for our food." "Now I lay me down to sleep…" These prayers were repeated so often they lost all meaning.

What if we used the same words in the same way, every day, when talking to the same person? They would probably think we aren't interested in communicating with them at an intimate level but are just going through the motions. Repetition in conversation isn't good enough for our earthly relationships, and it most certainly isn't good enough for our relationship with God.

In using repetition, or keeping our conversation with God at a general or repetitive level, we keep God at arm's length, not wanting to risk trusting Him with more specific prayers. To overcome this tendency, we need to think about the words we are saying, taking out the words we often tend to repeat (bless, watch over, take care of, lead…), and replacing them with more specific phrases.

Take a moment to consider your prayer life. Do you repeat the same words when you pray over a meal? Do your prayers for your family and friends sound the same every time you pray?

When you ask God to "bless" someone, how do you want His blessing? What is it what you actually want Him to do?

How can you reword your prayer for God to "bless" so it's more specific to the needs of the person or situation you're praying about?

How can you intentionally reword your daily prayers so they are unique to the situation, sincerely spoken to God, and not a repeat of what was spoken the day before?

Journal a prayer below for a blessing for someone in your life. Be specific and intentional in how you are asking God to bless them.

Sin

Sin is insidious. It makes its way into the depths of our being. Slowly our lives become nothing but one excuse after another as we lose our way and focus. It interrupts our connection with God, and prayer is our route back to Him.

We simply come to Him, sincerely and honestly. We don't have to clean ourselves up before we come to God. He's the one who does the cleansing.

Read Psalm 66:17-20.

List the things that the writer says about himself.

List the things the writer says about God.

Why does the writer say God heard and responded to his prayer?

What would hinder the writer's prayers?

What does this speak to your heart about sincerity and humility in confession and prayer?

When we come to God in confession and repentance, He hears us and continues the transformation.

THE SINFUL PRAYER

Does God hear the prayers of sinful people? If the answer is "no," then we are all hopelessly separated from Him.

2 Chronicles 7:14 is a call to prayer for God's people who have strayed from Him. Confession, through prayer, is essential for our prayers to be effective. As we seek Him and turn from our sin, He is present and ready to forgive, heal, and empower.

It's easy to convince ourselves that confession and forgiveness don't apply to us. Be forewarned, there were times shown in the Bible when God cut off communication with His children in order to get their attention and draw them back to Himself.

Read Joel 2:12-13. How does God say we are to return to Him after we have strayed?

Read Zechariah 1:3-6. What was the response of the people when the Lord said, "Return to me"?

Read James 4:8-10. How do these verses from the New Testament compare with the two previous verses from the Old Testament? Is there any differentiation in the way people are to return or draw near to the Lord?

When we come to the end of ourselves and surrender God picks us up and places us on the straight and narrow path. There is a divine initiative. We cry out to Him because He has drawn us to Himself. He convicts us of our sins and leads us to Himself in repentance. When we learn to overcome the hindrances to prayer, we will mine the treasures of the relationship we have built by spending time with our Abba, Father.

EXERCISES

1. Journal any hindrances you have to your prayer time and submit them to God. Be proactive about overcoming these hindrances.

2. How has focusing your prayer on God and the needs of others before your own needs changed your view of prayer? How has it changed the time you spend in prayer?

3. Work to make your prayer time a constant part of your day as you remember to have an ongoing conversation with God.

CHAPTER 5

BIBLE STUDY (OBSERVATION)

A friend told me about his family's favorite restaurant. I didn't recognize the name. When he told me where the restaurant was located, I realized I had passed the location many times. The next time I drove down the road, I looked, and sure enough, the restaurant was right where he said. It had been there for years. I just failed to observe it was there.

This happens all the time with Bible study, which is more than simply reading it. There's so much in God's Word. We can meditate, memorize, interpret, apply and obey it, as we dive into its depths and immerse in its teaching. A reward for this work is found in experiencing the growth God desires and it deserves our full attention.

Read 2 Timothy 2:15. In this verse, the Apostle Paul gave advice to the young preacher Timothy, telling him the foundation of his work was found in "the proper handling of God's Word." What do you think Paul meant by this phrase? For additional clarity, look up the following verses:

2 Timothy 3:14-16

JACK E. NEWTON

2 Timothy 4:2

Read Acts 17:10-11. How did the Bereans properly handle the Word of God?

How can we, as believers, be like the Bereans?

In this and the next two chapters, you will learn how to properly handle the Word of God through the Bible study method of observation, interpretation, and application.

Below are the benefits of studying God's Word. I have added a few illustrations to some of these benefits to help with your understanding. Add your own comments, stories, or notes to each bulleted item.

- It's pleasing to God.

    Ultimately, all of our motivations should be concerned with pleasing Him (1 Corinthians 10:31).

- It lights the darkness.

    When I was a child, I loved going to my uncle's lake cabin to fish and canoe. It was a boy's paradise. At night, my cousins and I would play hide and seek or capture the flag. One night, I was running in the dark. My foot stepped into a cattle guard and I took a nasty fall. It was only by the grace of God I didn't break my leg.

    This is similar to a Christian living in the world without the Word of God as a guide. All I needed was a light and things would have been different. The Word lights up the darkness and makes our way clear.

- To avoid error.

    It's easy to fall into error by pulling a verse out of context and manipulating it to say what we want it to say. With a book as extensive as the Bible, we can easily justify almost anything if we are willing to take it out of context. Therefore, we must be students of the Word and continually growing in our knowledge of the Scriptures as a whole. We also need to submit to others in the church and allow them to teach and correct us so we don't fall into error. Cults can start when one unteachable person develops a unique misinterpretation of a passage and persuades others to follow him or her.

- For right living.

    The Word of God matures and equips us to do those things pleasing to God. It corrects and disciplines us when we lose our way, and it sets us on the right path to serve and please God.

Athletes can have natural ability at performing their own specific sport. They train and they compete for the trophy. Without proper instruction and nutrition, there's just so far talent alone can take them. They do the best they can but they find themselves farther behind those who have great coaching and healthy nutrition. The Bible accomplishes both of these things and more in the life of a Christian. It's the coaching we need because all of our natural instincts are unproductive. Therefore, the Word prepares us to be victorious. It's also the nutrition we need to build our spiritual "muscles." Without it, we will never really be in the race.

The Process

Christians often attend a "Bible study," which is different from a church service. The Bible study typically uses a workbook for filling in the answers, and a group meeting where a learned teacher gives the correct answers. While these gatherings can be inspirational and helpful, rather than studying the Bible, the students learn from the study of others. Such courses can impact lives, but a greater impact comes when the student does their own search and struggle with the Scriptures.

To grow, we need to learn the process of studying the Word of God for ourselves.

Bible Study: Observation

In the 1980s, three-dimensional computer-generated art became popular. When you looked at the picture, it looked like a series of multicolored dots. The trick was to look at it properly. When you did, the dots became a three-dimensional picture of great detail.

My wife could easily see the hidden treasure within. I couldn't. I strained and stared but couldn't see anything except a series of colored pixels. I thought it was a hoax and no one could see anything except the dots. One day, I studied the picture, and with her coaching, I could see all sorts of things not visible before.

Many people feel that way when they read the Bible. They cannot see the meaning because no one taught them how to look. The process of Bible study helps us see what's there, by looking at the text.

- We must rid ourselves of personal bias and point of view.
- We must rid ourselves of preconceived notions and what we think it should say.
- We must put aside what we have heard about the passage from others.

GETTING STARTED | STEP ONE

To get you started learning the Observation, Interpretation, Application method, review the exercise included from Isaiah 6:1. If you prefer to do this in your journal, write the scripture text at the top of a page. Make a list of observations about the text. The order is unimportant. It can be rearranged later if needed.

This example gives an idea of a work in progress. It will be obvious that there could be many other observations made, questions asked, and applications applied. This is just a starting point.

In the year that King Uzziah died I saw the Lord sitting upon a throne, high and lifted up; and the train of his robe filled the temple. - Isaiah 6:1

OBSERVATIONS

- The time was in the year the king died.
- Uzziah was the king.
- He died.
- The verb tense is past.
- The author is remembering what happened.
- This is written in first person "I".
- This was a visual occurrence "I saw".
- The author saw the Lord.
- The Lord was sitting.

- He was sitting on a throne.
- The throne was high and lifted up.
- The Lord had a train.
- He was sitting in a temple.
- The train filled the temple.

EXERCISES

1. What's the difference between Bible reading and Bible study?

2. How can Bible study be of benefit in your Christian walk?

3. Begin your own Bible study. Read Isaiah 6:1-8 each day. Take one verse at a time and write as many observations as you can.

4. Were you able to see any things in the passage you might have missed if you just read it and moved on? What were they?

5. Why is the Observation step important in the process of Bible study?

CHAPTER 6

BIBLE STUDY (INTERPRETATION)

We have a fundamental misunderstanding of the step of interpretation of scripture. We don't need to know what a specific scripture means to us individually. We need to know what it means, period. The Word is from God, so we need to know what He meant when He inspired the writers to pen it. To apply the Word, we must understand what it meant when it was written to understand what it means today.

To understand the meaning of a passage, we cannot assume to know the answers. We must ask as many questions as we can about our observations, and let the answers lead us to the meaning. We do this by asking the basic who, what, when, where, why, and how questions. The more comprehensive our questions, the clearer our ultimate understanding of the passage. Then we use the proper tools to find the answers.

Why is the Bible considered an objective tool for Bible study?

What role does history play in Bible study?

Why must a student of the Bible be a student of words?

What are some of the literary forms used in the Bible? Why is it important to understand which literary form is used in specific passages?

Explain how the Holy Spirit can be listed as an objective tool in Bible study?

It may seem strange to list the Holy Spirit under objective tools. Remember a few things. First, the term "tool" is not a good descriptor for the Holy Spirit because He is God. He isn't something we pull out of our toolbox when we need Him. The Holy Spirit is the continual presence of God in the life of believers. At salvation, the believer begins an eternal relationship with God. God gives His Spirit to the believer to bring about all the things in life necessary for growth. Therefore, Bible study is a primary way the Holy Spirit communicates with and matures Christians.

Second, it's important to remember, the Holy Spirit isn't going to lead us to do anything contrary to the Word of God. Therefore, it's vitally important to know and study His Word. It's easy to convince ourselves we are "following the leadership of the Spirit' as we excuse unbiblical and unchristian conduct in our lives.

Finally, it's important to understand, the Holy Spirit isn't divided. If two people seek direction from God on the same subject matter, the answer cannot go in two directions. If the two people aren't in agreement, one of them is wrong. Often, we use the Holy Spirit as an excuse for doing what we want to do. This is a grave error. We cultivate a relationship with God through His Spirit and are continually filled with Him as we walk with God (Ephesians 5:18).

It's impossible to do the work of Bible study properly without the leadership of the Holy Spirit to help, guide, and correct us. We aren't merely studying ancient literature. We are seeking to understand the unique Word of God. Therefore, we begin with and rely on the Holy Spirit.

BASIC RESOURCES

List the basic resources available for Bible study.

Why is the concordance used as the primary resource for the definition of words and word meanings in the Bible?

What is the difference between a technical and devotional commentary?

Though a technical commentary is a great tool for interpretation, what warnings should a student of the Bible should be aware of in using the commentary as a primary resource?

A Word of Warning

My son often came home from school with statements of fact about one issue or another. When we asked him where he got his information, his reply was, "Matt told me." We loved Matt, and he was a great kid, but he wasn't an authority on anything. For years, the running inside joke in our family has been, "Well, if Matt said it, it must be true!"

Remember, a devotional commentary is the opinion of one person. This doesn't make it wrong, but it also doesn't make it correct or complete. It's easy to skip the steps of observation, interpretation and application and go directly to the commentary, but this leads to lazy Bible study and can lead to error. To properly handle the Word of God, we need to examine the Scriptures to find the true meaning, rather than depending on the interpretation of someone else.

GETTING STARTED | STEP TWO

The next step in the Observation, Interpretation, Application method, is to develop interpretive questions that go along with the observations made in Step one from the previous chapter.

INTERPRETIVE QUESTIONS

Remember, our interpretive questions will only be as good as our observations. As we develop the list of questions, we begin the process of digging for answers, which help us understand the meaning of the passage. The idea of a personal meaning isn't our goal. We're seeking to find <u>the</u> meaning, not merely <u>a</u> meaning. Interpretation is an art and a science, it's a skill developed over time, and we are able to see God work through us as we seek to understand His message.

> *In the year that King Uzziah died I saw the Lord sitting upon a throne, high and lifted up; and the train of his robe filled the temple. - Isaiah 6:1*

OBSERVATION	INTERPRETIVE QUESTION
The time was in the year the king died.	Why isn't there a more definitive date given (month, day, etc.)? What's significant about the year? Why is it important to equate the vision with the death of the king?
Uzziah was the king.	Of what was he king? How long did he reign? Was he a good or bad king? What does the name Uzziah mean?
He died.	How did he die? How old was he when he died? How did his death affect his people? What were the long-term implications of his death?
The verb tense is past.	What does this tell us about the observations he makes? How is the verb tense relevant to the event he witnessed? What does the past tense mean in Hebrew?
The author is remembering what happened.	What are the implications of using his memory? Does this shed any light on why he equated it with the death of the king? Does this give or take away from the validity to the vision itself?
This is written in first person "I".	Is the first person usually used in Hebrew writing? What's the significance of this point of view? Is Isaiah the author?
This was a visual occurrence "I saw".	Was this a vision? Was he really there? What's the meaning of the word "saw"?
The author saw the Lord.	Why is it significant that he saw the Lord? What does the Bible say about seeing the Lord? How did others react when they saw the Lord?

The Lord was sitting.	What is the significance of Him sitting?
	Does His placement rally matter?
	What are other examples of God sitting in the Bible?
He was sitting on a throne.	What's the significance and implication of a throne?
	Is there a comparison with king Uzziah here?
	What does the Bible have to say about God sitting on a throne?
The throne was high and lifted up.	Is this different from any other throne? How?
	What's the difference between "high" and "lifted up"?
The Lord had a train.	What is a train?
	Did every king have a train?
	Is this a cultural attire or a symbol?
	Is this literal or descriptive language?
He was sitting in a temple.	What is this temple?
	Where is this temple?
	How did Isaiah know it was a temple?
The train filled the temple.	Is this literal language or descriptive?
	Why is it important that His train filled the temple?

Each of the observations lead to many interpretive questions; we could ask many more than listed above. Once we have the questions, it's time to dig into the available tools to find the answers. Remember, some answers may be readily available, and some may take time to investigate. Others may never be answered this side of heaven. The struggle and the study are the important things. God will guide us if we allow Him.

EXERCISES

1. How is this process of Bible study different from the way you determined the meaning of the passage in the past?

2. Why is it important to shy away from a personal meaning?

3. Make a list of the interpretive tools you have. Make a list of those you would like to purchase in the future. Consider which, if any, software package you would like to purchase, or create a wish list and let your family and friends know of your need.

4. Take your list of observations from Isaiah 6:1-8 and ask as many interpretive questions you can think of, based on these observations.

5. Take one question at a time and investigate to find the answers.

6. How has this helped you understand Isaiah 6:1-8? How has your understanding of the meaning changed?

CHAPTER 7

BIBLE STUDY (APPLICATION)

Application occurs when we bring biblical truth into a present-day context in such a way that active obedience is the result.

Read Matthew 7:21-27. What do these scripture verses say about someone who doesn't obey the Word of God?

Read Colossians 2:6-7. What do these scripture verses say about someone who walks in obedience to the Word of God?

Read John 14:15. What does obedience to the Word of God say about your relationship with God?

Our salvation is based in a relationship with God, and this relationship is shown by our obedience. Therefore, we take the meaning we find in God's Word and put it into action. As we incorporate obedience into our daily lives, we become established in the faith. It isn't enough to intend to do the right things; we must follow through.

AUTHORITY IN THE LIFE OF BELIEVERS

When <u>tradition</u> is the source of authority in the life of a believer, anything threatening that tradition is seen as evil or unchristian.

> "Pastor, I cannot believe we're singing these new songs in church. If it isn't in the Hymnal, it's wrong," the man in my office shouted as his face became redder. I handed him my Bible and said, "Show me where that's found in the Word of God and we will never sing another song that isn't in the hymnal."
>
> In frustration, he took the Bible and said, "I'm not sure where, but I know it's in here. I heard a pastor say that if it isn't in the hymnal then it isn't of God." He looked through the Bible for a few minutes, and then out of frustration, threw it down and stormed out of my office, slamming the door as he went.

Tradition has a strong hold on many of us. We like to be comfortable and we like to do things the way we've always done them. Traditions based in the Scriptures are fine but all others must be challenged.

What other traditions do Christians cling to in order to feel secure in their faith and belief?

Examine your heart. Do any of these traditions have a strong hold on you?

<u>Experience</u> takes authority in the life of the believer when we follow how we feel, what we know, or what we have encountered.

When my son was in college, an acquaintance sent him an email. Though not verbatim it was something like this:

> Sam, God wants me to tell you something. He wants you to go overseas as a missionary. You need to stop running and submit to His call. Even though your parents are against you being in ministry, you should follow what God wants. I will be praying for you. In Christ, Joe.

Sam called to discuss this email. He knew his mother and I had prayed since before his birth that he would go into the ministry. "Should I take this seriously?"

"The answer depends on what you hold as authority in your life. If experience is your authority, then this is a real and powerful experience. However, if Scripture is the authority, then consider the teaching on prophecy. A prophet who actually speaks for God will always be correct. His prophecy will come to pass.

If it doesn't, then the prophecy isn't from God. In the Bible there were many times people claimed to be speaking for God but they weren't."

When my son heard this, he realized half of this "prophetic" email was wrong. It claimed his parents were against him being in the ministry. Sam made an appointment to meet with Joe. He explained how the message couldn't be from God because it contained falsehoods. Sam thanked him for His prayers, but he also made it clear that if God wanted to talk to him, He would do it in keeping with His Word.

Read Deuteronomy 18:22. How does this scripture point a Christian away from the authority of experience to the authority of God's Word?

Read Matthew 7:15-20. How do these verses encourage us to put the authority of God's Word over the authority of experience?

<u>Scripture</u> is the only trustworthy authority. If our tradition is contrary to the Word, our tradition must be changed. If our experience is contrary to the Word, the Bible takes precedence.

Read Jeremiah 17:9. How does this scripture confirm that God's Word is the Authority in our lives over tradition and experience?

PRINCIPLES OF APPLICATION

Why is it important to prayerfully seek the help of the Holy Spirit to find the correct response in applying scripture to our life?

Why is it important to do the hard work of observation and interpretation before moving directly to application?

Why is it important to steer away from comparing our life and behaviors with other people?

What happens when we willfully and truthfully look in the mirror in search of our inner self?

A young man came to discuss his recreational use of marijuana. He showed me Genesis 1 where God gave people dominion over all His creation. He logically explained that, since God gave people rule over creation, then smoking marijuana was affirmed within the teaching of God's Word. He didn't want to talk about what the rest of the Bible teaches about not being under the control of any mind altering or addictive substances. He didn't want to discuss how some things in creation, such as tobacco or poison, are actually detrimental to the health and welfare of people.

How did the young man try to manipulate scripture to justify his behavior?

Remember the example of biblical context from Chapter 5 that says, "A text without a context is a pretext." The Bible isn't just a series of random thoughts thrown together without intent. Every passage has been placed where it is for a specific reason. Each passage is observed in relation to its immediate context and relation to the Bible as a whole. With that in mind, let us do some investigative work in regards to this story.

Read Ephesians 5:18. How does this verse expose God's truth versus the young man's justification?

Read Galatians 5:19-21. How do these verses align with God's desire for us to be healthy and live abundant lives?

How would you have responded to the young man whose text was a pretext?

Though this is an extreme example, it's important to understand that our application must be in context with the biblical context. Therefore it cannot be applied in a way contrary to the clear teaching of Scriptures elsewhere.

GETTING STARTED | STEP THREE

The next step in the Observation, Interpretation, Application method, is learning how to apply scripture to current day life.

INTERPRETIVE ANSWERS

Choose a format helpful to you. This example from a study in Isaiah 6:1 is to give you an idea of a work in progress. It will be obvious that there could be many other observations made, questions asked, and applications applied. Remember, this is just a starting point.

> *In the year that King Uzziah died I saw the Lord sitting upon a throne, high and lifted up; and the train of his robe filled the temple. - Isaiah 6:1*

Here are the first two observations and their questions with the accompanying answers. Often the answers lead to more questions. For example: Why does Uzziah have two names? As we answer the questions, we begin to understand the meaning of the text. Next we must take the meaning and apply it to our lives today.

Observation 1:

OBSERVATION – The time was in the year the king died.	
INTERPRETIVE QUESTIONS	INTERPRETIVE ANSWERS
Why isn't there a more definitive date given (month, day, etc.)?	Isaiah used the year of the death of the king in other testimonies (Isaiah 14:28-32, for example).
What's significant about this year?	The specific date wasn't important to the point Isaiah was trying to make.
Why is it important to equate the vision with the death of the king?	The importance was to the death not the date. Uzziah died after a long reign and yet God's reign will never end.

Observation 2:

OBSERVATION – Uzziah was the king.	
INTERPRETIVE QUESTIONS	INTERPRETIVE ANSWERS
Of what was he king?	He was king of Judah (2 Kings 15:13; 2 Chronicles 25:27-26:1)
How long did he reign?	He reigned for 52 years (2 Chronicles 26:3)
Was he a good or bad king?	For the most part he was a good king, but he didn't take down the high places. He also became proud. (2 Kings 15:1-4; 2 Chronicles 26)
What does the name Uzziah mean?	He was given leprosy for his disobedience. (2 Kings 15:5-7; 2 Chronicles 26:1-23) The name Uzziah (Yahweh is my strength). He was also called Azariah (Yahweh has helped).

Application is where the rubber meets the road in Christianity. It's where the Word is taken off the written page and lived out. We depend on the Spirit of God to lead us and keep us from error. The process of Bible study is foundational to our growth in faith.

Personal application to scripture will be directed by the Holy Spirit, and will be unique to each person's situation and place in life. As an example of personal application, one person may hear the following from the Holy Spirit in how to apply the truths found in Isaiah 6:1.

- My life is filled with worry, anxiety and fear. In this study, I see that I don't need to worry about my life, my resources, or my country because God's reign will never end. He will always hold control over the earth.

- Being a Christian who is somewhat obedient isn't the same as being someone who walks in obedience. I want to be able to look in the mirror and see the high places in my life where I hold idols in my heart, and break those down.

- I don't want pride to reign in my life. I want to walk humbly with God.

- God will deal with those who walk in disobedience. I want to live with open ears and an open heart so I understand and obey the Word of God.

- God is my strength and my helper. I can call on Him in times of need.

EXERCISES

1. Why is application important in the life of a believer?

2. How can the step of application be misunderstood?

3. Why are we tempted to skip straight to application without doing the other phases of Bible study?

4. After you finish with the observation and interpretation work on Isaiah 6:1-8, journal one personal application from the truths in the passage each day for one week. Incorporate these applications in your daily life.

CHAPTER 8

CHURCH MEMBERSHIP

Because of the way they have been treated, many Christians don't see the need to be a member of a church. Christians have a reputation for kicking each other when they are down. Where did this reputation come from? For the most part, we have earned it. However, much of what has been said about Christians has been taken out of context and many unfair accusations have been cast at us.

Mainline denominations are seeing declines in membership, attendance and baptisms. Sermons can be read in books, watched on television, and heard in podcasts. Christian music is available over the internet or radio. A great many Christians, especially younger ones, don't see the need for the church, and many churches don't emphasize or require attendance or membership.

Is the church an institution that has outlived its usefulness?

Is it time to do away with the church?

Read John 13:35. How can the church remedy this situation?

Now that you have given your opinion, let's take a look at the biblical function of the church.

THE UNIVERSAL CHURCH

The universal church refers to the whole company of regenerate people regardless of their denomination, place in history, or geographic location. It's made up of all the believers everywhere and from all time. Ignatius of Antioch declared, "Where Jesus Christ is, there is the catholic church."

"I believe in … the holy catholic church"

This line in the Apostles' Creed is confusing to many people. The Apostles' Creed is an early statement of Christian doctrine that is embraced by many Christians today. This particular line doesn't refer to the Roman Catholic denomination. The "c" is lower case in catholic. This word means "comprehensive or universal." The Catholic Church is often called the "universal church" or sometimes the "invisible church."

Understand, the Apostles' Creed didn't come from the original twelve Apostles. In fact, the doctrine of the universal church only came into existence in the second century. The biblical basis for this doctrine is found in the New Testament.

THE LOCAL CHURCH

The local church is the visible church. Most references to the church in the New Testament refer to a local body of Christ, which is located in a specific geographic location and refers to the people and not a building.

The church is a body that's made up of many parts, with each member having a specific purpose to fulfill, and the members are baptized believers. Church membership is only available to believers.

THE IMPORTANCE OF THE LOCAL CHURCH

1. People need people.
2. The church needs each member.
3. Christ is the head, creator, and sovereign.
4. The church is God's plan for those who have a relationship with Christ.

Read 1 Corinthians 12:12-27. What is the importance of each member?

Read 1 Corinthians 3:10-11. What is the importance of how we build the foundation of the church?

EXERCISES:

1. Why is church membership essential to spiritual growth?

2. What hinders people from joining a church?

3. How is a biblical view of the local church important when it comes to church membership?

4. Are you a member of a local church? If not, why? Are your reasons biblical? Ask God to lead you to the church He has for you. Begin (or continue) attending a Bible believing church.

CHAPTER 9

Purpose of the Church

The primary function of the church is to carry out the Great Commission. Another function is to properly and biblically administer the ordinances of the Lord's Supper and baptism. From the beginning, the local church has been associated with these two ordinances.

Read Matthew 28:18-20. List the four directives given to disciples of Jesus:

1.

2.

3.

4.

What words are used in the above verse that teaches us we aren't only tasked with evangelism, but also discipleship?

Read 1 Corinthians 11:20-26. What instructions does Paul give the church in administering the Lord's Supper? What correction does he give?

One day at the gym, I introduced myself to someone I hadn't previous met. Almost immediately, we knew we were Christian brothers. We spent the next hour sharing what God had done in our lives and praying. This is an example of Christian fellowship; relating to others under the lordship of Christ. Have you had a situation where you met someone and knew right away they were a believer? Describe the connection you had at the time of the first meeting.

Read Acts 2:44-46. How has the modern day church relinquished its responsibility to the government in some areas?

How can the modern day church return to being like the church mentioned in Acts 2:44-46?

There are both privileges and responsibilities of being a member of a church. How is a believer to view their role and responsibility in church membership? Give one or two examples of how you serve within your local church for each of the categories listed below.

1. Serve Others
2. Attendance
3. Accountability
4. Discipleship
5. Belonging
6. Giving

If you are lacking in any of these areas of responsibility, what is holding you back?

How can you overcome these distractions or hindrances, so you are doing your part within the body of believers?

Attendance

One of the primary responsibilities of the church member is attendance. Today most churches are satisfied if 50% of their members attend on any given Sunday. This is a sad commentary on the state of the church and a fundamental reason why many Christians aren't growing in their faith.

There's no way to be a part of something in that we don't participate. The idea of making church attendance mandatory is almost unheard of today. However, there was a time in the not too distant past, when attendance was the primary responsibility of the church member and memberships were revoked for non-attendance. This extreme may not be necessary, but there is nothing wrong with having high expectations for church members.

What if you were a member of the early church and you decided to sleep in on the first Pentecost? Or the day Peter preached and 3,000 were saved? Or the day Eutychus was raised from the dead? Or the time Paul and Barnabas reported on their missionary journey? You cannot predict which Sunday is going to be "the" Sunday. You cannot expect spiritual growth without being in regular and faithful attendance to the church to which you belong.

Accountability

We need one another in order to grow. The church is a place of accountability. There are people in the church who love us enough to expect us to behave in a Christian manner and love us enough to bring to our attention those areas of our lives needing work. For example, Paul confronted Peter when he refused to eat with Gentiles (Galatians 2:11-13).

One man described his accountability group at church as the place where men go to lie to one another and convince themselves nothing is wrong with them. This obviously isn't an example of biblical accountability. In order to be accountable to one another, we have to be teachable and honest with each other. The church is where we find empathy for our struggles and also discipline for our sin.

CHURCH MEMBERSHIP

Church membership is important to grow in our walk with Christ. The church needs each of its members, and each member needs the church. We need one another for growth.

If you are looking for a church home, listed below are some questions you can ask before becoming a member, to help discern if it's the church God is calling you to join.

- What does your church believe about the Bible?
- What does your church believe about salvation?
- Who is God?
- Tell me about the history of your church.
- What is the mission/vision of the church?
- How is the church involved in the local community?
- How is the church involved in international missions?
- What portion of the membership is actively serving in ministry?
- Does your church practice church discipline?
- How can I (and my family) contribute to the church fulfilling its mission?
- Are there resources available to help my children to grow in the faith?
- How long has the pastor been here?
- What type of preaching does the pastor use?
- Are there any other offices in the church (deacon, elder…)?
- How are decisions made in the church?
- Are there small groups/Sunday school where we can get to know people more intimately?
- What is the process for becoming a member?

REASONS TO LEAVE A CHURCH

Obviously, this isn't an exhaustive list. The important thing to understand is, leaving a church is a serious decision to come to only after prayerful consideration.

Orthodox, biblical theology is no longer being taught or preached in the church. This doesn't mean the preacher said something with which we disagree. There are plenty of areas where Christians disagree. There are however, some areas of theology that are non-negotiable. If false doctrine is being taught as truth or biblical doctrine has been abandoned, then it's appropriate to consider leaving.

There are no opportunities to serve. A few years ago a friend was serving in a large church in North Texas. She built a ministry to women and was leading Bible studies for over 500 women each week. It was decided only staff members could lead ministries in the church. Since all the staff were men, this all but nullified her ministry. The staff informed her she could no longer use the church building for women's Bible studies and she could no longer be the leader since she wasn't on staff. It became apparent there was no longer a place of service for her at the church. After prayerful consideration, she and her husband quietly moved to another church where she could serve.

The church is unwilling to discipline moral failure according to the teaching of the Scriptures, especially in leadership. Many churches have abandoned discipline in the name of tolerance and love. Many moral failures have been covered up or simply ignored. This cannot be allowed to stand, particularly when it comes to those in positions of leadership within the church.

There are legitimate concerns for the safety of children. If there are actual situations that put our families at risk, then leaving is appropriate.

God is leading us to leave. I include this reason with trepidation. Sometimes God will lead us to a new place of service. He may have something He wants us to do and someone He wants us to reach. I don't believe however, God leads us to a church and then He leads us away two or three months later. If we find ourselves repeating, "God told me to leave," over and over, we might need to examine our hearts to determine if we are just using God to justify our actions. God desires for us to face and deal with our problems rather than run from them. We are God's instruments. He isn't ours.

JACK E. NEWTON

REASONS NOT TO LEAVE A CHURCH

Here are some that aren't legitimate reasons to leave.

- Things have changed.
- Someone hurt my feelings.
- The pastor preaches too long.
- I don't like the music.
- The preacher doesn't wear a suit and tie.
- The preacher started using a different version of the Bible.
- They use overhead projectors instead of hymnals.
- There is no choir.
- I left, and no one tried to come talk me out of it.
- The church is reaching out to people with which I would rather not associate.
- They sing more choruses than hymns, or vice versa.
- The church won't let me designate my offerings wherever I want it to go.
- They are using drums in the worship service.
- They require a new member's class.
- The pastor is a good preacher but not really a pastor.
- No one came to see me when I was in the hospital.
- They don't have the Lord's Supper every week.
- The pastor wore jeans.
- I didn't get to sing a solo.

EXERCISES

1. What is the importance of church in the life of a believer?

2. Journal your thoughts on responsibilities and privileges you see in church membership.

Chapter 10

Church Discipline

One of the most important aspects of church membership is church discipline, which has all but been abandoned by the modern-day church, much to its detriment. When we understand we are responsible for and accountable to one another, church discipline is necessary and expected.

Too often, when we are hurt by someone in the church we vent our frustrations and hurts to others. This gossip doesn't solve anything; rather, it makes matters worse. Much of the friction and difficulty within the church could be avoided if we talked to one another rather than talking about one another.

Read Matthew 18:15-17. What are the four steps the church is told to practice when someone within the church sins against another believer?

1.

2.

3.

4.

When these steps aren't taken in church discipline, what is the detriment to the church and the community?

What's the purpose of church discipline?

Read Matthew 18:17b. What did Jesus mean when He said to treat the person as a Gentile or a tax collector?

Read Romans 10:1, Acts 26:16-18, and Colossians 4:5-6. What should a Christian's attitude and actions be toward those who don't know the Lord? Why do we often fall short of this teaching?

In 2 Corinthians 2:2-10, how is the church told to respond to the repentant man who had been excluded from the church through church discipline?

How does this example and teaching about church discipline encourage you?

Why is church discipline important?

Why do churches shy away from church discipline?

CHAPTER 11

CORPORATE PRAYER

any churches in our culture don't see the hand of God moving among them because they are prayerless individually and corporately.

Years ago, I was the youth pastor of a church with a crumbling parking lot. The deacons met and decided it was long overdue for the church to repave the lot. They got bids and decided the church should take out a $25,000 loan to accomplish the needed repairs. They brought their proposal to the church and it was expected the church would automatically approve the direction of the leaders.

Before the vote, a lady asked how many had given this idea any prayer. She talked about the serious nature of going into debt and wondered if it was God's will. We realized we hadn't prayed about the issue nor asked God what He wanted. It was such a practical thing we assumed it had to be His will. After she spoke, the pastor asked the church to table the motion for one month so we could see God's plan. Everyone left with the conviction to pray. We prayed alone and we prayed together. Before the end of the month, more than $25,000 had been given to the church as extra offerings. We were able to get the parking lot repaired without taking out a loan.

Things happen when God's people pray. There is something powerful about the people of God putting aside their own agendas and coming together to seek and do the will of God.

JACK E. NEWTON

TEACHING ON CORPORATE PRAYER IN THE BIBLE

Read 2 Chronicles 7:14. Who is God addressing in this verse?

According to this scripture, what is the role of each believer in preparation for corporate prayer? Notice how different this teaching is from the way we often pray together. Here, the central focus is on an intimate relationship with God rather than our own self-interests and our ailments.

Read 2 Chronicles 16:9. Who is the Lord seeking? What does He want to provide?

When my daughter was young, she found out she could get me to do things for her if she crawled into my lap and asked me in her sweet little voice. There were limits to this, of course, but she often tried to use this method to get her way. When we treat God in this way, we don't understand His true nature. We think we must manipulate God's heart toward us. It is already there. We simply turn to Him and when we do, we find He is ready to give us what is right.

In your personal prayer time, do you often try to manipulate God into doing your will? Take your time in answering this question. Often our manipulation attempts are second nature and we don't realize the depth of our motivation in attempting to get what we want rather than yielding to His will.

Read Matthew 18:19-20. What happens when God's people are gathered in His name?

What does it mean to be gathered "in His name?" See Exodus 3:13-18, Psalm 68:4, and Zechariah 10:12 for further study.

Read John 14:13. What does it mean to ask "in His name?"

Read 1 Timothy 2:1-4. We are admonished to pray for those in authority. The key to leading a life pleasing to God is to pray for those in earthly authority over us. As we submit to them we also submit to God. Who has God placed in your life as an authority figure? How do you rate your ability to submit to those in authority in your life?

Having an understanding that submitting to those in authority is submitting to God, does this change your attitude or view of those who are in authority? Do you pray for them?

Read James 5:14-16. The power of God's people praying has great impact and invites Him to work in our midst. Are you willing to participate in corporate prayer for the needs of others?

In 1 John 5:14-15, we read, "if we ask anything according to God's will, He will hear us. And if we know that He hears us in whatever we ask, we know that we have the requests that we have asked of Him." How do you know this isn't a free-for-all wish list that will be granted as if God were a genie in a bottle?

Many years ago, I met a man who bragged God was going to give him a brand new Mercedes. He quoted these verses, "God hears me and He will give me whatever I request." At the time, I didn't know enough to ask him if having this new luxury car was God's will. As far as I know, he is still waiting for his new car.

Scripture gives us confidence that our prayers have an impact on our world. However, God's will is supreme. We know when we submit to His will, He hears and answers us. We cannot manipulate God into giving us what we want; we submit to Him and we ask according to His will.

What does it mean to ask in accordance with His will? Read Jeremiah 42:1-3; Romans 8:27, Colossians 1:9, and James 4:3, for further study.

In a day and age when the world is at odds with God and His ways, the need for a godly example is all the more necessary. The book of Judges shows a pattern in the history of Israel. The Israelites followed a particular judge and served the Lord as long as the judge lived. Then they fell away, worshiping idols and neglecting the true God. To draw them back, God brought judgment in different forms (drought, war, famine…). They then came together and cried out to Him, repenting of their sin and turning toward God. This rollercoaster was perpetuated by the corporate sin of the people and their need to humble themselves and come before God corporately for forgiveness and renewal.

What is the difference in personal prayer versus corporate prayer in the aspect of corporate confession?

In corporate prayer, confession is admitting what we, the church or the group, have done we shouldn't have done and those things we haven't done that we should have. This is corporate confession, not individual confession.

TYPES OF CORPORATE PRAYER

CONCURRENT CORPORATE PRAYER

This occurs when each person in a prayer meeting prays, out loud, at the same time. My church has a prayer meeting on Wednesday evenings following our Bible study. We break into small groups and pray as the Lord leads. It's a wonderful, special, and powerful thing, to hear a room of God's people speaking with their Lord. The murmur of those prayers, though I usually cannot distinguish any distinct words in the midst of it, have a very special impact on this pastor's heart.

CONSECUTIVE CORPORATE PRAYER

Consecutive prayer occurs when each person prays in turn, listening to the prayers of others, and praying when it's their turn. It's important to remain focused on the Lord throughout the process, especially in taking prayer requests. There's a fine line between a prayer request and gossip. Often the prayer request time is used as an opportunity to talk about others in unacceptable and unchristian ways. We need to examine our motives and our heart. It's easy for corporate prayer meetings to devolve into gossip sessions or simply listing our physical ailments. It's better to err on the side of caution and silently pray, than using our prayer request time to share private issues of someone else's life.

CONVERSATIONAL CORPORATE PRAYER

This type of prayer follows a set pattern and a conversation with God. No prayer requests are taken, but the conversation is guided by the pattern used. The pattern is an effective and helpful model. The components are praise, thanksgiving, confession, intercession and supplication. There is no set order in how the participants pray, they contribute a one or two sentence prayer on the topic. The conversation with God is a natural extension of the way we normally interact with others. Below is an example of conversational corporate prayer.

Conversational prayer is a powerful experience for a prayer group. It's hard to imagine how it sounds in practice because it's so different from the way we normally pray together. Here's an example of four Christians (Jon, Sam, Leah, and Dana) praying together, using conversational prayer. Dana is the leader in this example.

Dana: God we come together, and we want to begin by PRAISING You.

> Sam: God You are great.
> Leah: Father You are beyond our ability to describe You.
> Sam: What is man that You are mindful of Him?
> Jon: You are the King of Kings.
> Dana: God You are my all in all. Everywhere I go I see You.
> Leah: Jesus You are my Savior, Redeemer, and Lord.

Dana: God we have so much to be THANKFUL for. Thank You for a new day to walk with You.

> Jon: Thank You for saving me Lord.
> Leah: Thank You for Jesus. For the empty cross and the empty tomb.
> Jon: Thank You for the way You spoke to me in church yesterday.
> Sam: Thank You Lord for being with me in my job interview last week.
> Jon: I'm so grateful for the family You have given me, Lord.
> Dana: Thank You for providing a new youth pastor for our church.

Dana: Lord we readily CONFESS we aren't all we need to be.

> Jon: God we have been complacent about evangelism. Please forgive us Lord.
> Sam: God please intervene in the lives of those who's hearts are hardened to the Gospel and your Word.
> Leah: Lord You know our church has an issue with Gossip. Forgive us Lord.
> Dana: Yes Lord. Let us talk to one another instead of talking about one another.
> Jon: God You know our hearts. We fall short in many ways. We need You Lord.

Dana: Father, we want to INTERCEDE for those in need in our church.

> Sam: Lord please be with Mrs. Jones as she has surgery today.
> Leah: Yes Lord, she is very afraid. Calm her heart.
> Dana: Help us to remember to visit her and take a meal by her house.
> Jon: I lift up the folks in the apartment complex where I live. There are so many there who don't know You Lord. Help us reach them.
> Sam: Show us how we can minister to these people more effectively.
> Leah: God, we know You love them. Help us to have Your heart for them.

Dana: We now come before You in an act of SUPPLICATION, asking You to meet our needs. God please help Sam to get the job he interviewed for last week.

> Sam: If this it's Your will for me Lord I want it. If not, lead me to the job You have for me.
> Leah: Please help me to deal with my coworker in a way which will honor You. You know we don't always get along.
> Dana: Help Leah to remember she is Your representative wherever she goes. Use her in this person's life.
> Jon: I am going out of town on business next week Lord. Please watch over my family while I am gone.

Sam: God we know You love Jon's family even more than we do, so we trust You with their well-being. Give Jon peace as he travels, knowing You will take care of things beyond his reach.

Dana: We thank You we have had the privilege and opportunity to spend this time with You. Thanks for hearing our prayers. Amen.

EXERCISES

1. Are you willing to pray with other Christians? If not, what is keeping you from corporate prayer? Seek God and the advice of mature Christians to help you overcome your reluctance.

2. Seek out a group of Christians to pray with on a regular basis.

3. Ask your group if they would be willing to learn conversational prayer. If so, teach them the pattern and how to incorporate it.

4. What hindrances have you encountered in corporate prayer? Ask God to help you overcome these hindrances.

5. Add any prayer requests from your corporate prayer time to your journal and pray for them privately as well.

CHAPTER 12

WORSHIP

"What type of worship do you have in your church?" This is often a question people ask when they hear I'm a pastor. They are usually asking about the type of music we have in our worship services. While music is an important aspect of worship, it's by no means all this word conveys. Worship is far more than a music style. It encompasses our entire approach to the righteous and holy God of the universe.

Elements of Christian worship consist of prayer, music, preaching, giving, and the ordinances of baptism and the Lord's Supper, to name a few.

ELEMENTS OF CHRISTIAN WORSHIP

P<small>RAYER</small>

Corporate prayer is one of the most powerful elements in Christian worship. In prayer, we cry out to God and seek to hear from Him. A disturbing trend in modern-day worship is the removal of prayer from the worship service. The church needs God and therefore, the church must seek to communicate (speak and listen) with Him when they are gathered in His name. If not, the focus turns to areas other than God's will. This is a dangerous place for a church to find itself.

JACK E. NEWTON

What are the dangers of removing prayer from corporate worship? List as many as you can think of.

How can the church protect the element of prayer during times of meeting together for worship?

The prayer of a righteous man is powerful and effective (James 5:16). Journal a prayer below, expressing your concern for prayer to be protected within the body of believers.

MUSIC

Most people equate worship with music. Music has a powerful impact on our lives. When I hear a song I haven't heard in a while, I remember every word. Such is the lasting impact of music. It imbeds itself into our lives in ways nothing else can.

Music can also divide people due to opinions and preference, which can also be felt in worship music. Some Christians believe certain worship music is acceptable and other music is out of bounds. When new songs and styles are introduced, they are often met with resistance. The resistance is often based in personal preference, tradition, and comfort rather than Scripture.

Churches have fractured and many bad feelings have been harbored over the topic of music. Remember, worship is focused on God. Therefore, the factor which needs to be considered is whether the music is in keeping with the teachings of the Word of God and brings glory to Him. For example, many older conservative Christians are more comfortable with the song *Have a Little Talk with Jesus* than they are a new hymn like *In Christ Alone* even though the first song talks about the unscriptural "prayer wheel" and the second is very sound theologically. There are also many examples of shallow contemporary songs as opposed to older hymn that are deep and rich. Newness or oldness aren't the factors which make the difference. Is it sound doctrinally? Does it focus on bringing glory to God?

Newer songs are often called "7-11 music." Seven words repeated eleven times. While some criticism of mindless and seemingly endless repetition is appropriate, many of the songs that have been effective through the ages have used repetition. "Holy, Holy, Holy," is repeated with vigor and strength as we sing the powerful hymn with the same name. It's counterproductive to reject all new music and accept all older music, or vice versa. God has given us more wisdom and discernment than that. When we evaluate music not in our preferred genre, we see there is much good in the new and the old. God is the focus of worship. Therefore, the factor to consider is whether the music keeps with the teachings of the Word of God and brings glory to Him.

I heard an elderly preacher say, "Much of the newer music isn't what I'm used to. In fact, I don't like much of it, but a few Sundays ago, I sat with my grandchildren and I saw them singing and worshiping the Lord to a song I didn't know. This brings a smile to this old preacher's heart. Then I realized it wasn't about me. I realized God was calling me to give rather than to take, so my grandchildren and their generation could know my God." This is the attitude we all need, young and old. It isn't about us.

When music is used to worship God, it takes on an important role in our lives. Is there a song that ministers to you each time you hear it? Explain.

What is the importance of worship music keeping with the teachings in Scripture?

What is the role of music in our corporate worship and our individual worship?

Preaching

Much of what passes for preaching today is merely an attempt to manipulate the Scriptures to say what the speaker wants to say. In this method, the preacher is in command and he determines how to use the Scriptures to say what has already been predetermined as the topic. The preacher is the authority and the Bible is a tool used to communicate the will of the preacher. While this may bring attention and praise upon the speaker for being eloquent or clever in manipulating the Word, it isn't biblical preaching.

The difference between topical and expository preaching is more than splitting theological hairs. These involve fundamentally different approaches to God and to the Word of God. If we believe the Word is authoritative in our lives, it impacts how we handle, study, and preach. We are then able to communicate God's message to others.

At a pastors' conference Alistair Begg once told me to focus on "Systematic Consecutive Exposition of the Scriptures."

- Systematic: Bible study determines the meaning of the text, the meaning is communicated to the church, and applications and illustrations are drawn from the meaning.

- Consecutive: we preach the books in the manner in which they are written, line by line, paragraph by paragraph, chapter by chapter, and book by book. This gives preachers freedom, because they don't have to figure out what passage they should use each Sunday. Instead, they make their way through the book at hand in the order in which it was written. This communicates to the church that the Word is the authority. It also forces the preacher and the church to deal with difficult passages. Often the Bible doesn't tell us what we want to hear, but it always tells us what we need to hear.

- Exposition: reveals the meaning of the Scriptures to the people. This type of preaching is vital to true worship. Only it can make sure the focus is on God where it belongs.

Therefore, expository preaching is used powerfully by God to help Christians grow in their walk with Him.

EXERCISES

1. How is worship today different from the early church?

2. What needs to change about our worship to align it with the teaching from Scripture?

3. What is the proper role of the clergy in the worship of the church?

4. How can we help others in the church understand and participate in their role of worship?

5. What hindrances have you encountered in worship? Are these based in Scripture or personal preference? Ask God to help you overcome them.

6. What should be our approach to music used in worship?

7. Why is expository preaching needed and necessary for Christian growth?

CHAPTER 13

EVANGELISM

INVITATION

When I was a new Christian, I went to an old-fashioned tent revival. I loved the music and the preaching. I was like a sponge absorbing everything. One night the preacher gave a seemingly endless invitation. I desired to be obedient to everything and anything the Lord wanted me to do. So, a few minutes later, I found myself at the altar along with dozens of people. The preacher then led us to pray the sinner's prayer. I was already saved! I knew it. But somehow I had been manipulated into walking down the aisle. It left a really bad taste in my mouth because I felt I had been tricked. Since then, I have been observant of how invitations are conducted. I found some of them are manipulations of people and not a movement of God. This is a shame and isn't what God intended.

Should we do away with invitations completely? Just because some abuse and misuse it, doesn't mean we should abandon it. We wouldn't do so in other areas of our Christian walk.

How can invitations (altar calls) be conducted in a way that honors and depends upon God?

Your Salvation Testimony

When the Apostle Paul was imprisoned and given a chance to defend himself, he continually went back to his salvation experience as his defense (Acts 22:6-16; 26:12-18). Our testimony is an important and powerful tool God can use to convince others of the truth of the Gospel. It also helps us remember who we were before we came to know God and the wonderful things He has done. This keeps the work of God fresh in our mind and helps us not take His grace and mercy for granted.

Personal Salvation Testimony

Writing our testimony helps us examine, polish, and refine the message of our personal salvation experience. It also helps us remember what God has done and examine our salvation to make sure it's firmly based in biblical teaching and not in the tradition or desires of people.

Answering three questions will guide us in developing a succinct and powerful testimony.

1. <u>What was my life like before I came to know Christ?</u>

    This answer helps others see we aren't perfect. We all have struggles. These difficulties are part of life. The sad thing is we often try to deal with our issues without the Lord's help. We don't need to go into all the details about our life before conversion. In fact, too much detail can distract from the message we want to convey.

    It's important to guard against romanticizing sin. We can paint a picture of what our life was like without embellishing the story to make sin look desirable. Sin is real, so communicating how it negatively impacted our life is critical.

It's also possible to convey the emptiness, lostness, and purposelessness of life before we came to Christ in just three or four sentences.

2. <u>What were the circumstances of your salvation experience?</u>

The answer to this question is vitally important. Whenever we meet a new couple and attempt to get to know them, we ask, "Where did you two meet?" Some answers to this question are short and sweet, while others are complicated. Every relationship has a beginning point. Some of us know the exact date we yielded our life to Christ. Others may only remember the situation and events of salvation. The date isn't as important as the actual circumstances surrounding our conversion experience.

God uses people to share His Gospel with others. Share who He has used in your life. What were the circumstances surrounding your conversion? Were you in church? A hospital? Your living-room? Why were you brought to a point of decision at this time?

Answers to these questions help explain the experience. It's important to remember God is the focus, not self. Try to communicate this information in three or four sentences.

3. <u>What has your life been like since you came to know the Lord?</u>

There is a temptation to end our testimony with our salvation experience. But something that happened years ago has little value to someone currently wrestling with the Gospel. It's powerfully effective to tell them how God has changed our life since our conversion. When we communicate not only what God did for us, but also what He is currently doing, we bring our salvation into the present and our relationship with God becomes alive and powerful to others.

As we read the New Testament, and especially the book of Acts, we see followers of Christ sharing what God did in their life. Today, our world is skeptical of spiritual things. We can help overcome this skepticism as we testify about God's work.

Again, this doesn't have to be a long historical treatise. We aren't the focus, but we endeavor to show the great things God is doing. This can be shared in three or four sentences. We need to update our testimony regularly to keep it current and relevant.

JACK E. NEWTON

Tips on Writing and Sharing Your Testimony

First, <u>shorter is better.</u> While many people might find a short (1 to 3 minute) personal story interesting, they are usually not going to sit still for a thirty-minute sermon. Even if they are too polite to leave, chances are they will mentally check out long before we finish. It's better to start with a short testimony than to bore them to the point of losing interest altogether.

Second, <u>avoid using "churchy" words.</u> Christians have a vocabulary that isn't easily understood by those outside the church. While we may be excited we have discovered the meaning of "propitiation" or "atonement," these words have little or no impact on the unbelieving world. We cannot assume people know the meaning of even simple Christian concepts.

In this post-Christian culture, many of the words we use are foreign to the thinking of the world at large. This makes defining our terms necessary. Even a simple word like "sin" needs to be explained in its biblical context and in a way easily understood by our hearers. It's our responsibility to communicate clearly and on a level people can understand.

The Gospel message stays the same, but we can express it in different ways. Paul used different words to talk to the Jews in Jerusalem (Acts 22) than he did to the Greeks in Athens at Areopagus (Acts 17). An understanding of our audience influences how we communicate in ways that convey the truth of the power of God's Gospel to change lives.

Third, <u>show the written testimony to a mature Christian.</u> We need to draw upon one another to grow and be strengthened in our Christian walk. A second set of eyes on our testimony keeps us from errors. Ask for help to improve it. Solicit questions they anticipate might be asked and seek help in developing clear responses. Because communication is a difficult process, often what we mean to say is miscommunicated when we put it into writing. Ask for help to avoid this pitfall.

Fourth, <u>practice.</u> Once the testimony is written and the message is satisfactorily communicated, it needs to become part of who we are. It isn't just a story on a piece of paper. It's YOUR story. Take it to heart and practice sharing it with others.

Finally, we can <u>look to God</u> to provide opportunities to share our testimony. Before beginning, ask for permission to share. This shows courtesy to the listener without the perception you are trying to push or sell something.

SAMPLE TESTIMONY

This sample testimony answers the following three questions:

1. What was my life like before I came to know Jesus Christ?

2. What were the circumstances of my salvation experience?

3. What has my life been like since I came to know the Lord?

When I was younger, I spent my life trying to fill the emptiness inside with everything the world had to offer. The more I tried, the emptier I felt. In fact, I convinced myself what I had was as good as life could get.

Then, I met a Christian. She seemed to have a peace and contentment I couldn't attain in my own life. She told me about Christ and His love for me. I asked a lot of questions and looked honestly at myself for the first time. I realized she was telling me the truth, and it was what I had been looking for. So, one day I got on my knees and placed my faith in Christ. He saved me that day. I was twenty-five years old.

Since then, my life hasn't been perfect. I have made many mistakes and suffered many heartbreaks. But little by little, I have grown in the Lord. He has provided me with a family and a purpose. I know when my time comes to leave this life I will spend eternity with Him.

Questions to Start a Spiritual Conversation

Moving a conversation to spiritual things takes a little finesse and intuition. These reminders will serve you well as you listen and wait for the right opportunity to ask questions that will redirect the conversation.

- Remember, look for opportunities to move any encounter in a spiritual direction.

- Remember, look for a natural flow in the conversation to ask questions. If questions come out of the blue, they won't be effective.

- Remember, be respectful of those encountered. Ask for permission to share, be sensitive to feelings and body language, and be more of a listener than a talker.

EXAMPLES

Below are questions to help redirect a conversation to spiritual things.

- Where do you go to church?

- What are your feelings about church?

- What is the most important thing in your life?

- If you were on an island and could only take two things with you, what would you take?

- I was reading the Bible today; can I share what I learned?

- Have you ever read the Bible?

- What person has had the most influence over your life? Why?

- Is there anything I can pray for you about?

- What happens to a person after they die?

EXERCISES

1. Write your testimony. Describe your life before you knew Christ. What were the circumstances of your salvation? What has your life been like since you came to know Christ?

2. Show your written testimony to a mature Christian and ask for their feedback. Use their input to make your testimony more effective.

3. Practice sharing your personal testimony in front of a mirror to make sure delivery is natural and sincere; work to make it a conversation rather than a sales pitch or an acting job. Then, go to the person who helped with the written version and role-play. Ask them to play the part of the intended audience and ask tough questions in response. Don't be concerned about knowing answers to their questions. "I don't know," is a perfectly valid answer. Rehearse your testimony until it naturally flows.

4. Ask God for opportunities to share your testimony.

5. After sharing your testimony, journal your experience. Was it effective? What was the response of the listener? Did they have questions? Were you able to answer them? Are there questions you need to research? (If you question your effectiveness, don't let fear of failure prevent you from trying again.)

The Plan of Salvation

If you're uncertain about your relationship with God, please consider what He is saying to you in this example. When you are ready to place your faith in Christ, please see the sinner's prayer later in this chapter.

If you're using this in order to learn to share the Gospel, understand that it isn't meant to be memorized and recited. This is a tool for becoming a more proficient evangelist.

EXAMPLE OF SHARING THE GOSPEL

The Gospel begins with an understanding of sin. Everyone is a sinner (Romans 3:23). This means everyone has done something wrong they fall below God's standard of perfection. It's easy to compare ourselves to other people. You might look pretty good compared to me, but this isn't the standard. We must compare ourselves to the sinless perfection of God. When we do, it's easy to see we don't measure up. Would you admit you have sinned at least once in your life?

Next, sin comes with a penalty. Scripture says, "The wages of sin is death" (Romans 6:23). Death in the Bible is separation from God. It includes separation here on earth, where we're unable to find the fulfillment and purpose for which we were created. It also includes separation in eternity. A wage is something we earn. When we allow sin into our lives, we earn death.

All this is bad news. Here is the good news! God understands our predicament. We are sinners, and our sin separates us from Him. No matter how many good works we do, we cannot wash away our sin. This is where God stepped in and provided a way. He loves us so much, He came to the earth as a man to take our place (John 3:16). If death comes because of sin, then why did Jesus die? He had no sin. He was perfect and sinless. The answer is, He took our place. He took our punishment. He loves you that much, which is pretty good news, right?

Well, most people have heard that Jesus died for our sins. What they often don't understand is, just knowing about Jesus isn't enough. The Bible says even the demons believe God exists (James 2:19). Salvation is about more than merely believing God exists. It's about responding in faith to the offer of salvation God has provided through Jesus (This is a good place to insert your personal testimony by asking, "Would it be all right if I share what God did for me?"). God loves you and wants you to find forgiveness and new life in Him. Is this something you are interested in? Do you have any questions?

The Sinner's Prayer

The "sinner's prayer" is a powerful way a person can respond and accept the Gospel message of Jesus. Remember, these aren't "magic words." This is an example of the sinner's prayer that may be used.

Dear God,

I know I am a sinner. I have done many wrong things. My sin separates me from you. I also know You love me and You showed Your love when Jesus died on the cross for me. Today I believe with my heart and confess with my mouth that Jesus is my Savior and Lord. Thank you for loving me and providing this forgiveness and eternal life I couldn't provide for myself. May my life bring glory to You. In Jesus name. Amen.

SCRIPTURE REFERENCES FOR THE PLAN OF SALVATION

ALL HAVE SINNED

The Bible teaches, every person is a sinner. (Genesis 6:11-12; Judges 21:25; 1 Kings 8:46; Job 15:16; Psalm 14:1, 3; 53:1, 3; 143:3; Ecclesiastes 7:20; Isaiah 53:6; Jeremiah 30:14-15; 32:30, 32; Zechariah 5:6; Matthew 7:11; 15:28-29; Luke 11:13; Romans 3:10, 23; 6:17; Galatians 3:22; 2 Thessalonians 2:3; 2 Peter 2:4; 1 John 3:8)

SIN SEPARATES PEOPLE FROM GOD

Since we are all sinners we have earned separation from God. This separation occurs while we are on earth but continues into eternity. (Isaiah 59:2; Romans 6:23a; Galatians 5:4; Ephesians 2:12; 2 Thessalonians 1:9)

JESUS LOVES SO MUCH HE DIED FOR ALL

Jesus loved the sinful world so much He died on the cross in the place of all sinners. He provided the only way of salvation for the lost world. (Isaiah 53:6; John 3:16; 14:6; Romans 5:8; 2 Corinthians 5:15, 21; Hebrews 2:9; 9:26-28; 10:10; 1 Peter 3:18; 1 John 2:2)

BELIEF (FAITH) IN HIM PROVIDES ETERNAL LIFE

Only a faith response to the Gospel message results in eternal life. Good works (religion, charity, piety…) won't save us. Only faith in Jesus Christ results in a personal relationship with Him. (John 3:16, 36; 10:26-30; 17:3; Acts 2:21; 22:16; Romans 6:23; 10:9-10, 13; Galatians 6:8; Ephesians 2:8-10; 1 Timothy 1:16; 1 John 5:13)

JACK E. NEWTON

EXERCISES

1. What hinders you from sharing your faith?

2. What role does evangelism play in the everyday life of the ordinary Christian?

3. How does evangelism contribute to Christian growth?

4. How can you as an individual and we as a church be more evangelistic?

5. What is the name of a lost person you can reach out to? How can you develop a relationship with them?

6. What can you do to begin meeting and developing relationships with lost people?

7. What books can you read to improve on evangelism? Is there another Christian you can ask for help? Who?

8. Pray daily for opportunities to share your faith.

9. Are you familiar enough with your personal salvation testimony to share it when the opportunity arises? If not, practice and ask for the help of others.

CHAPTER 14

MINISTRY

When Dana and I were dating, we worked in a bus ministry that brought hundreds of children to church on Sunday. We taught the 4-year-old class. I was a new believer and eager to learn and serve. What could a person possibly get from teaching a bunch of toddlers? It turned out to be one of the most rewarding experiences of our lives. We had so much fun teaching the Bible to kids in a way which made it easy for them to understand. I was hooked. From then on I looked for places to serve.

Sometimes church members are referred to as "the frozen chosen." In fact, we have accepted the rule that 80% of the work is done by 20% of the people. This is a shame. Not only does it contribute to the decline and ineffectiveness of the local church, but it also cheats the vast majority of Christians of the blessings of service. Think about a body that is 80% paralyzed not due to a disease, but due to choice. This would be a pitiable shame, yet it's the situation we have accepted as normal in many of our churches today. No wonder Christians aren't growing and finding the joy God has for them. If we're going to turn this trend around, we need to become a serving people. We were created to serve God and we serve Him by serving others. This is the only way we can fulfill our created purpose (Ephesians 2:10).

Why are only 20% of the people actively serving in the church?

Why are we willing to accept this?

What are the long-term implications for the church if this trend continues?

SERVICE

When I met John, he was retired and a deacon in the church where I served as youth pastor. I loved to arrive to church early on Saturday morning to finish preparing for Sunday, because it was quiet with no one around. Almost every week I would look out my office window and see John mowing the church lawn. John had a bad back and was struggling with several other health issues. I asked, "John, why don't you let some of us younger guys mow the lawn? You don't need to be out here in the Texas heat doing this."

John looked at me with fire in his eyes. "You can't take this away from me. It isn't a chore to me. It's one of the ways I serve the Lord and I look forward to being out here each week."

This is one of the many lessons John taught me. I never thought of mowing the church lawn as a ministry, but it was the thing that energized John and he continued to do it for years.

What are some ways that you can serve the Lord?

What hinders you from service?

To Encourage Other Believers

> *And he gave the apostles, the prophets, the evangelists, the shepherds and teachers, to equip the saints for the work of ministry, for building up the body of Christ, until we all attain to the unity of the faith and of the knowledge of the Son of God, to mature manhood, to the measure of the stature of the fullness of Christ. - Ephesians 4:11-13*

After reading Paul's message to Timothy, we might be tempted to think service is only for pastors like Timothy. Paul made it clear when he wrote to the church in Ephesus this wasn't the case. In fact it was the role of the church leaders to equip the church members to do the work of the ministry. Therefore, the bulk of the ministry of the church is meant to be accomplished by the members of the church.

HOW CAN WE SERVE?

Most churches are desperate for people to serve in their differing ministries. We can ask God to show us a ministry in our church or community that meets our interests and gifts and then volunteer to help.

Serving within the authority of the church allows us the protection, resources, and guidance God provides the church.

We shouldn't worry about serving in the wrong area. God will show us what to do and empower us to do it. Remember, we aren't called to do what we can, but to do more than we can. We are called to accomplish what only God can do through us.

When we're serving, we grow. The teacher always learns more than the student. The one who visits folks in the hospital in order to be a blessing, is always blessed in the process. Those who give to help others, find they are blessed in the giving.

We won't be successful in every endeavor. Growth comes through failure as well as success. In fact, we cannot really fail as long as we're being obedient to God's leadership in our lives.

EXERCISES

1. Why is it important for Christians to serve?

2. What are the benefits of Christians in ministry?

3. Why are Christians reluctant to serve?

4. How does Christian service impact the lost world?

5. How has God gifted you?

6. How can you serve God, your church, and your community?

7. Are you willing to serve? If not, why? Ask for God's help to overcome these issues.

8. Do you know anyone who needs your help in their Christian growth? What are some ways you can assist them?

END NOTES

Overview – Companion Workbook

[1] Card, Michael, and Thompson, John W. <u>Joy in the Journey</u> lyrics ©Warner/Chappell Music, Inc.

SUGGESTED READING

Each of these books contributed directly or indirectly to the writing of this work. I recommend reading good, solid books to assist you in continued spiritual growth. This list is just the beginning and in no way is an exhaustive list of good books available.

Anayabwile, Thabiti M. *What is a Healthy Church Member?* Wheaton, IL: Crossway, 2008.

Ashcraft, Morris. *Christian Faith and Beliefs.* Nashville, TN: Broadman Press, 1984.

Basden, Paul. *The Worship Maze: Finding a Style to Fit Your Church.* Downers Grove, IL: Intervarsity Press, 1999.

Bettenson, Henry. *Documents of the Christians Church.* New York: Oxford University Press, 1963.

Blackaby, Henry and Richard Blackaby and Claude King. *Experiencing God: Knowing and Doing the Will of God.* Nashville, TN: Lifeway Press, 2007.

Bolt, Peter and Mark Thompson. *The Gospel to the Nations.* Downers Grove, IL: Intervarsity Press, 2000.

Bonhoeffer, Dietrich. *Life Together.* New York: Harper and Row, 1954.

Bounds, E. M. *Power Through Prayer.* Chicago: Moody Press, 1979

Bradshaw, Paul. *Early Christian Worship.* Collegeville, MN: Liturgical Press, 1996.

Bright, Bill. *Witnessing Without Fear.* Nashville, TN: Thomas Nelson, 1993.

Cairns, Earle E. *Christianity Through the Centuries.* Grand Rapids, MI: Academie, 1954.

Carson, D. A. *Worship by the Book.* Grand Rapids, MI: Zondervan, 2002.

Chan, Francis and Danea Yankoski. *The Forgotten God.* Colorado Springs: David C Cook, 2009.

Chan, Francis and Danea Yankoski and Chris Tomlin. *Crazy Love.* Colorado Springs: David C Cook, 2013.

Chan, Francis and Mark Beuving. *Multiply: Disciples Making Disciples.* Colorado Springs: David C Cook, 2012.

Coleman, Lucien E. *How to Teach the Bible.* Nashville, TN: Broadman, 1979.

Coleman, Robert E. *The Master Plan of Evangelism.* Grand Rapids, MI: Fleming H. Revel, 1963.

Corley, Bruce and Steve Lemke and Grant Lovejoy. *Biblical Hermeneutics: A Comprehensive Introduction to Interpreting Scripture.* Nashville, TN: Broadman and Holman Publishing, 1996.

Crawford, Dan. *Discipleshape: Twelve Weeks to Spiritual Fitness.* Peabody, MA: Hendrickson, 1998.

Cymbala, Jim. *Fresh Wind, Fresh Fire.* Grand Rapids, MI: Zondervan, 1997.

Dever, Mark. *Nine Marks of a Healthy Church.* Wheaton, IL: Crossway, 2004.

Enns, Paul. *Approaching God.* Grand Rapids, MI: Kregel, 1991.

Fee, Gordon. *New Testament Exegesis.* Louisville, KY: Westminster John Knox Press, 2002.

Fee, Gordon D. and Douglas Stuart. *How to Read the Bible Book by Book.* Grand Rapids, MI: Zondervan, 2002.

Feldman, Adam L. *Journaling: Catalyzing Spiritual Growth Through Reflection*. Ellicott City, MD: Milltown Publishing, 2013.

Foster, Richard. *Celebration of Discipline*. San Francisco: Harper, 1998.

Frame, John M. *Contemporary Worship Music: A Biblical Defense*. Phillipsburg, NJ: Presbyterian and Reformed Publishing, 1997.

Gilbert, Greg. *What is the Gospel?* Wheaton, IL: Crossway, 2010.

Goldsworthy, Graeme. *Christ-Centered Biblical Theology*. Downers Grove, IL: Intervarsity Press, 2012.

Gonzalez, Justo L. *The Story of Christianity, Volume 1*. New York: Harpersanfrancisco, 1984.

Groeschel, Craig. *The Christian Atheist*. Grand Rapids, MI: Zondervan, 2010.

Hendricks, Howard G. and William D. Hendricks. *Living by the Book*. Chicago: Moody Press, 1991.

Hobbs, Herschel H. *Getting Acquainted with the Bible*. Nashville, TN: Convention Press, 1991.

Hughes, R. Kent. *Disciplines of a Godly Many*. Wheaton, IL: Crossway, 2001.

Hunt, T. W. and Catherine Walker. *Disciples Prayer Life: Walking in Fellowship with God*. Nashville, TN: Lifeway Press, 1997.

Hurtado, Larry W. *At the Origins of Christian Worship*. Grand Rapids, MI: William B. Eerdmans Publishing: 1999.

Keller, Timothy. *The Reason for God*. New York: Dutton, 2008.

Klug, Ron. *How to Keep a Spiritual Journal*. Minneapolis, MN: Augsburg Fortress Publishers, 2002.

Leeman, Jonathan. *Church Discipline*. Wheaton, IL: Crossway, 2012.

Little, Paul. *How to Give Away Your Faith*. Downers Grove, IL: Intervarsity Press, 1988.

Lloyd-Jones, D. Martyn. *Preaching and Preachers*. Grand Rapids, MI: Zondervan, 1971.

MacDonald, Gordon. *Ordering Your Private World.* Nashville, TN: Thomas Nelson Publishers, 1984.

MacDonald, James. *Lord Change My Attitude (Before it's too Late).* Chicago: Moody Press, 2001.

Martin, Glen and Dian Ginter. *Power House: A Step-By-Step Guide to Building a Church that Prays.* Nashville, TN: Broadman and Holman Publishing, 1994.

McBeth, Leon H. *The Baptist Heritage.* Nashville, TN: Broadman Press, 1987.

Moore, Beth. *Praying God's Word.* Nashville, TN: Broadman and Holman Publishing, 2000.

Olson, C. Gordon. *Getting the Gospel Right.* Cedar Knolls, NJ: Global Gospel Publishers, 2002.

Packer, J. I. *God's Words.* Grand Rapids, MI: Baker House Books, 1981.

Piper, John. *A Hunger for God.* Wheaton, IL: Crossway, 1997.

Rainer, Thom S. *I am a Church Member.* Nashville, TN: B & H, 2013.

Ravenhill, Leonard. *Revival Praying.* Minneapolis, MN: Bethany House Publishers, 1962.

Reid, Alvin. *Evangelism Handbook.* Nashville, TN: Broadman and Holman Publishing, 2009.

Robinson, Darrell W. *People Sharing Jesus.* Nashville, TN: Thomas Nelson Publishers, 1995.

Sanders, Oswald. *In Pursuit of Maturity.* Eastbourne: Kingsway Publications, 1985.

Searcy, Nelson and Jennifer Dykes Henson. *The Difference Maker.* Boca Raton, FL: Church Leader Insights, 2016.

Segler, Franklin M. *Christian Worship.* Nashville, TN: Broadman and Holman Publishing,

Tchividjian, Tullian. *Do I Know God?* Colorado Springs, CO: Multnoma, 2007.

Thompson, Oscar W. and Carolyn Thompson. *Concentric Circles of Concern.* Nashville, TN: Broadman Press, 1981.

Tozer, A. W. *Whatever Happened to Worship?* Camp Hill, PA: Christian Publications, 1985.

Traina, Robert A. *Methodical Bible Study.* Grand Rapids, MI: Francis Asbury Press, 1952.

Welch, Bobby H. and Doug Williams. *A Journey in Faith.* Nashville, TN: Lifeway Press, 1998.

White, James F. *Protestant Worship.* Louisville, KY: Westminster John Knox Press, 1989.

Whitney, Donald S. *Praying the Bible.* Wheaton, IL: Crossway, 2015.

Willard, Dallas. *The Divine Conspiracy.* New York: Harpersanfrancisco, 1997.

ABOUT THE AUTHOR

JACK NEWTON has served in pastoral ministry for over 30 years. He has pastored churches in Texas, Maryland, and Oklahoma. This former Marine is a writer and speaker who has a passion for seeing people come to know and grow in Christ. He is currently serving as a Senior Pastor in Tyler, Texas where he lives with his wife of 34 years, Dana. Jack, a proud father of three wonderful children, enjoys spending time with his five grandchildren.

www.ingramcontent.com/pod-product-compliance
Lightning Source LLC
Chambersburg PA
CBHW060423010526
44118CB00017B/2338